The Colours of Virtue

Inspirational Stories and Meditations

Elizabeth Medler

This quietly uplifting compilation of inspirational meditations has evidently been composed with assiduous care. The book is simple in structure and unassuming in presentation, yet the work as a whole has profound substance in its assured tone of steady encouragement. The essential point is that it needs to be read and sampled slowly—then only can it work its quiet magic.

Upon each short chapter—with its themed tail-piece illustration with brief sentence for a moment of reflection—the author brings to bear her considerable philosophic learning and editorial expertise. The sober but engaging text is filled with the insightful wisdom drawn from her years as spiritual magazine Editor of *New Vision*, but the writing here is enlivened and made much easier to absorb by her skilful use of simple analogy and vivid anecdote, backed up by precise fact.

The end result is satisfying indeed. These thoughtful reflections carry the quiet power to still the wayward mind and ease the troubling anxiety of the heart, because they emerge from Elizabeth Medler's own deep understanding of what an authentic spiritual life requires by way of sincere commitment, together with a clear awareness of spirituality's rich promise as well as its hidden pitfalls.

Philip Pegler author of *Hidden Beauty of the Commonplace, Meeting Evil with Mercy* and *Quiet Courage of the Inner Light*
www.hiddenbeautyoflife.com

The Colours of Virtue

Inspirational Stories and Meditations

I ask you about Virtue and you present me with a whole swarm of them...
Socrates to Meno

Elizabeth Medler

St Ursin Press

First published in Great Britain in 2020
by St Ursin Press, 3 Broadfield Court,
1-3 Broadfield Road, Folkestone, Kent CT20 2JT, UK

© Elizabeth Medler.
The author asserts her moral right to be identified as the author of this work.

All rights reserved. No part of this publication may be reproduced, stored in a retrieval system, or transmitted in any form or by any means, electronic, mechanical, photocopying, recording, or otherwise, without the prior permission of the author.

We gratefully acknowledge the financial support of the Pelegrin Trust in the publication of this book.

Cover design: 'Kingfisher ~ Aflame-like beauty on the wing' by JL Walker © 2020

Set in Garamond 11.5

ISBN 978-0-9955730-6-2

St Ursin Press is an imprint of Trencavel Press
www.trencavel.co.uk/St Ursin.html

Dedication

I dedicate this book to all the beautiful souls who have shone light on my path and contributed richly to my life through their very being.

All these friends have, in a way, written this book. I would also like to especially thank:

The Fintry Trust
The School of Philosophy and Economic Science
Henry Thomas Hamblin
Arthur Farndell
Raymond Payne
Mary Spain
Anthony Werner

Contents

Foreword	1
Author's Note	3
Tales of Perseverance	7
Artist Souls at Work in the World	9
May We Prosper	13
The Joy of Giving and Receiving	15
Purity ~ Join Me in a Spiritual Shower...	17
Is There a Plan for our Lives?	20
The Healing Balm of Forgiveness	23
The Second Birth	27
Journey to the Centre of Ourselves	30
Follow the Pilot	33
The Law of Reciprocal Service	36
Courageous Living Always Speaks to Us	39
The Wisdom of the Sunflower	42
A Winter's Retreat	45
Lark Ascending	46
All Pervading Light	49
Present and Connected	52
Listening to the Still Small Voice	55

Perfect Order all Around	57
Taking the Colours of the Day back into the White Light of Eternity	60
The Power of Creative Thinking ~ Collaboration in the Aquarian Age	62
The Infallible Workings of Justice	65
Nourishing Our Whole Being	68
The Fountain of Life ~ Singing our Note	71
The Joy of Meditation	73
Finding the Divine by Accepting Ariadne's Golden Thread	76
A Rainbow of Abundance	79
Let's Say 'Yes' to Life	82
Flexibility	85

Foreword

To embark on writing a book about Virtue requires a dash of courage, a pinch of patience, and a sprinkling of justice, the whole dish to be marinaded in lashings of love and beauty. Our author is a homely, friendly companion, one we instinctively trust to lead us gently through time and space and offer us the spiritual nourishment we sorely need in our famine-stricken times.

She effortlessly evokes our own childhood by reminding us of our expeditions to catch cabbage whites and cage them in jam jars, our youthful fascination with the flight of birds and the miraculous growth of flowers, and our receptivity to the impressions wrought upon our young souls by the never-ending changes arising from the procession of the seasons. This very evocation challenges us all to become as little children once more, that we may enter the Kingdom of Heaven and actually perceive the reality of the universal Ideas of Unity, Goodness, Truth, and Beauty, with Love as the great connector.

As a young boy during the Second World War, I used to watch my mother prepare my favourite dish. We called it summer pudding. Although the ingredients were of the earth earthy—stale slices of bread and summer fruit—and were packed into a white earthenware bowl whose surface was crazed with a hundred fine cracks, the result came straight from heaven and was totally divine, a yearly miracle, which I relished half a teaspoonful at a time. This book reminds me of that summer pudding. The commonplace elements of mundane life—boarding a plane, watching a sunflower grow, seeing an apparently chaotic jumble in Truro Cathedral, observing a silver birch dancing in the breeze—are transformed by Elizabeth Medler's insights into miracles that open the heart. Her book is one to be savoured half a teaspoonful at a time.

Arthur Farndell

Author of:
How to be Top at Spelling
Succeed in Maths
A Mahābhārata Companion
Gardens of Philosophy
Evermore Shall Be So
When Philosophers Rule
All Things Natural
On the Nature of Love

Author's Note

In Plato's dialogue of the same name, Meno, a wealthy visitor from Athens, asks Socrates about the nature of Virtue. Whether it is acquired by teaching or by practice, or whether it comes to men by nature or in some other way. Socrates replies that he does not know what Virtue is. Turning the tables, Socrates asks Meno what he thinks Virtue is. Obligingly, Meno replies that virtues are numberless and have many definitions. He proceeds to describe a whole string of examples. Socrates replies: 'How fortunate I am, Meno! When I ask you for one virtue, you present me with a whole swarm of them...' It transpires that Socrates is looking for the nature of Virtue *itself*, rather than distinct virtues.

It cannot be denied, though, that by reflecting on a swarm of virtues, it may be possible to begin to see what is common to them all. It might be helpful, therefore, if you approach the short sketches in this modest volume rather like a bee, sipping nectar from each and seeing what they may have in common. This is to approach Virtue inductively, drawing on particular virtues to extract the essence of Virtue. We can also work the other way ~ deductively ~ drawing into our Centre and using our intuition to 'touch' the heart of Virtue. Once we have touched the essence, it might be easier to understand what makes any particular virtue a virtue. These approaches are complementary and, like a ladder, we can move upwards from the many to the one true essence and downwards from the one true essence to the many. But, however we choose to proceed, it is vital that we first ask for help from our guardian angel. Divine Grace always comes to assist us whenever we ask for it sincerely.

The cardinal virtues ~ Courage (or Fortitude), Temperance, Wisdom and Justice, will be familiar to most of us, but on the whole, although we may have witnessed some fine examples of these, we probably haven't thought about what they share in common. Even an enlightened soul, like Socrates, was inspired to explore the nature of Virtue throughout the whole of his life. By the end of the *Meno*, Socrates is still not sure about the essence of Virtue. What he does show is that Virtue cannot be taught (because it is not knowledge) and that it is probably given to the virtuous as a gift from the Divine. For anyone wanting to pursue this important subject further, it might be helpful to read Plato's dialogues, specifically *The Republic, Gorgias* and *Protagoras*.

Virtues have been called 'excellences' or 'perfumes' arising from living a *good* life ~ that is a fulfilled life where all potentials are fully actualised.

There are species of Virtue, just as there are species of birds or trees. These beautiful excellences are like adornments, bejewelling the soul at every level, and beyond, into her 'root' of pure Spirit. They range all the way up from the Physical and Ethical Virtues, to the Cathartic, Contemplative, Paradigmatic and Hieratic Virtues. It is not within the scope of this book to explore these individually, but we can safely say that through the virtues the soul becomes God-like.

The world's wisdom literature holds sacred the reality of the celestial hierarchies. These Intelligences are Divine and nine-fold. The Virtues are in the fifth place, the first being the Seraphim, followed by Cherubim, Thrones, Dominions, Virtues, Powers, Principalities, Archangels and Angels. It's interesting to see that the Virtues take a mid-way position within the hierarchy. The mid-way position is often honoured as the position of Soul between Spirit and Body, so possibly the Virtues are like the Soul of the Divine, but that is something for meditation...

The Divine Virtues are honoured in a most beautiful way in a book called *The Mystical Theology and The Celestial Hierarchies of Dionysius the Areopagite*[1]. The identity of the author, who calls himself Dionysius, is not known but it is thought he may have been a Syrian monk. In the book, the Virtues are named as *streams of life and love* and *assimilative spirits of purity*

Author's Note

and beauty. But, most importantly, the text touches on the *superessential Virtue* which is named the *Source* of Virtue which *flows providentially to those below it abundantly filling them with virtue.*

This book sketches some of the qualities and virtues we all need for living life well and coming closer to our own Self, whose raiment is pure white and yet contains all the colours of the rainbow. Each offering is accompanied by a meditation which I hope will go some way towards unfolding its significance and make it relevant to you. Rather than being read as a book from beginning to end in linear form, I hope you can dip into it as often as you like and let the page fall where it will.

This book cannot pretend to be a true study of Virtue as it concerns itself more with the swarm, but nevertheless it is offered as food for thought. I hope you enjoy it!

Elizabeth Medler
lillibet7@icloud.com

---

[1] *The Mystical Theology and The Celestial Hierarchies of Dionysius the Areopagite* translated from the Greek with commentaries by The Editors of The Shrine of Wisdom, Fintry, Brook, Nr Godalming, Surrey GU8 5UQ, ISBN 0 900664 03 7

Tales of Perseverance

It's not that I'm so smart, it's just that I stay with problems longer.

Albert Einstein

In 1985 Simon Yates and Joe Simpson successfully reached the summit of the West Face of Siula Grande in the Peruvian Andes. On their descent they ran into serious problems. Joe slipped and broke his right leg. Clearly, this was to make the descent very difficult indeed. Simon did his best to lower Joe off the North Ridge, but with storm conditions prevailing and darkness descending, Simon accidentally lowered Joe off a cliff. He could feel the whole weight of him on the rope but of course Joe could not climb up and Simon could not pull him back up. After considerable effort and deliberation, Simon cut the rope. Joe, by now suffering from hypothermia, plummeted down the cliff and into a deep crevasse. Simon descended the mountain but on reaching the crevasse, realised the gravity of the situation and naturally assumed that Joe had died. In fact Joe had survived the massive fall and landed miraculously on a small ledge inside the crevasse. Coming round, he realised the rope had been cut and he would have to save himself. Thus began the exhausting and treacherous journey down the mountain. Against the odds Joe reached the bottom and crawled and hopped five miles back to base camp reaching their tent just a few hours before Simon intended to leave. This is, of course, a grossly simplified version of Simon and Joe's epic tale as set out in Joe's gripping book and film, *Touching the Void*. It is an outstanding representation of the important quality of perseverance without which little can be achieved. And in some extreme cases, such as the one recounted, lives depend upon it.

The Colours of Virtue

We all have to persevere in spite of, or sometimes because of, extremely trying conditions. Indeed, so often when our circumstances are tough or challenging in some way, we are more likely to persevere. We are also more likely to persevere when we envision a goal ~ something we really want to achieve. In Greek mythology Penelope exercised perseverance in a creative way and because of this she was reunited with her husband, Ulysses. The story begins when Ulysses was called to the Trojan war and was not expected to return alive. Penelope was besieged by suitors all of whom wished to marry her, but she longed only for her husband to return. She began to weave a robe for the funeral canopy of Laertes, her husband's father, pledging that when it was complete she would choose a suitor. However, during the day she wove but at night she undid the work so it was never completed! She persisted in this art until at last Ulysses returned, vanquished all the suitors and reclaimed his wife.

> *Pause*
>
> Whenever you feel overwhelmed, take one step at a time and persevere.

Penelope weaves a splendid robe

Artist Souls at Work in the World

As lovers of life, we can use each moment as a doorway into the timeless Now of eternity. If we are fully present, we begin to really notice the beauty all around and entering into it, we find that we have left time behind and entered into an altogether different realm. It is the Master Jesus who reminds us that there are many mansions in the Divine Kingdom ~ all to be enjoyed, they serve to raise our perspective so that we are no longer limited by time, space and circumstance. It is equally true that the key to each kingdom lies within, but the corresponding 'mansion' or 'room' will not be revealed to us until we have earned the right to enter. To enter anything, we have in some sense to become like it. It is said that whatever we repeatedly contemplate, we tend to become like, so let us contemplate the Divine within ourselves and within all things.

In Alice in Wonderland the white rabbit rushes by: 'I'm late, I'm late, for a very important date ~ no time to say hello goodbye...' I wonder, are we that white rabbit always in a rush with no time to spare, no time to just be; no time to do what people used to call 'passing the time of day'; no time to ponder the beauty all around and to see the Angels that William Blake saw in the trees?

If we are always eager to move on to the next thing, we have no time to enjoy the 'Now', no time to really listen to family, friends, neighbours, the man in the subway, the stranger. If we cannot give ourselves to the 'Now', how can we be present enough to really enjoy life?

Sometimes we become preoccupied with capturing life through the lens of a camera or phone. Whilst this is understandable, because we want to treasure our memories (and the photo is a symbol of the experience), there is also a danger that in our rush to freeze the moment, we miss its full import and divorce ourselves from the 'presence' of the moment which cannot really be captured.

Birthdays, weddings, holidays ~ in short, celebrations of all kinds ~ all have a timeless quality. Why, I wonder? Possibly happiness (and any strong feeling) outweighs the passing of time. Next time you are really focussed on something, notice that time no longer seems to exist. It may be a platitude to say, 'time flies when we are enjoying ourselves' but it is nonetheless true. Remember William Blake's words: 'He who kisses the joy as it flies lives in eternity's sunrise'? Eternity's sunrise is the Timeless Now. We enter it by savouring the moment and, as it were, lightly kissing it rather than trying to 'grab' it or own it for ourselves. Do you recall catching 'cabbage whites' in your net as a child and then quickly transferring them into a jar with holes in the top? If so, like me, you were doing the reverse of kissing the joy ~ you were actually trying to bottle it and keep it for yourself ~ as if something so rare and so beautiful, whose very purpose it is to fly, should be trapped and caged. This action is a graphic symbol of humanity's desire to acquire and the gluttony, avarice and possessiveness which stem from it. Every time we try to 'own' something for ourselves with no intention to share it, it is as if we are not only catching a butterfly but pinning it to a board, just as we might see in any natural history museum. Many of us want to take those pins out and let the butterfly soar to its home in the natural heavens.

Time is like the net in which we caught our butterfly ~ if we are not careful, we can become trapped in it rather than use it to our advantage. How to get out of the net? Perhaps the first major step is to realise that the aspect of us called 'Spirit' can never be caught by a net because it transcends it, enjoying a freedom beyond words to describe. And yet Spirit has tremendous compassion for the ego (the part of us that wants to 'own' and looks for reward) which invariably becomes entangled in the net. When faced with a personal problem or knot, we often panic and the knot we are trying to undo becomes worse! The best way forward is to sit completely still, focus intently and clearly on the problem, perhaps framing it as a question to ourselves, and then offer it up to the Divine to address. Because we are wont to worry about our problems, it requires tremendous faith and trust to completely let go. As the Divine Sees with unobscured 360 degree Vision, nothing is hidden. That great One Knows what is best. If we are receptive and still, opening our souls to receive, a ray of light will appear to illuminate our Way. This may come when we least expect it.

Eternal Ideas and virtues like Temperance, Fortitude, Wisdom and Justice are timeless and dwell permanently in the Now. As human souls we are asked not only to appreciate the timeless nature of these Ideas and virtues but we are called to unfold them in time. This is no easy task ~ it is rather like putting the proverbial 'quart into a pint pot'! This is why artists (and we are all artists in the sense that we all create) are invariably disillusioned by their creations as they never seem to correspond to the beauty and perfection they see in their mind's eye. The truth is that we cannot fully express what we see in the Timeless Now into time. 'Time,' said Plato, 'is a flowing image of eternity.' In other words, the image is not the reality, but rather its shadow. For all that, some images are more beautiful than others in that they reflect more of Beauty herself. By understanding this, we can relax more knowing that our creations can only approximate to what we see inwardly. But this doesn't mean we should stop honing our skills and making our creations more and more like those perfect Ideas we can see in our mind's eye. And not only this... it is also true to say that when we give our ideas form by manifesting them in some way, we perform a valuable service, actualising what was before only potential. Moreover, by expressing our creativity and giving it form, we inspire others to be creative also and so several beautiful fruits can develop from one fruit. The world's great creations are often brought into being by several souls ~ each putting in place a vital aspect. The following popular proverb demonstrates what happens when we fail to contribute our share.

For want of a nail the shoe was lost.
For want of a shoe the horse was lost.
For want of a horse the rider was lost.
For want of a rider the message was lost.
For want of a message the battle was lost.
For want of a battle the kingdom was lost.
And all for want of a horseshoe nail.

> ## Pause
>
> *'I'm late, I'm late for a very important date. No time to say hello, goodbye, I'm late…'* Today make time to be present to each person you meet.
>
>

May We Prosper

Every thought that you have impacts you. By shifting from a thought that weakens to one that strengthens, you raise your energy vibration and strengthen yourself and the immediate energy field.

Dr Wayne Dyer

Recently, whilst leafing through one of my old notebooks, I came across some hastily scribbled words I rather like: *If you separate yourself from God in thought, you will also separate yourself from Him in manifestation.* (This is undoubtedly true because action follows thought.) The same author goes on to say: *I have been shown that when man thinks on a plane with pure spirit, the soul enters consciously that realm where it perceives the ideal of things rather than the things themselves.* It strikes me that this Consciousness (capital 'C') is the abundant or prosperous Consciousness in which we come close to the *isness* or essence of things in the Mind of God. There is no paucity There. In his *Book of Daily Readings* for January 31, the 20th century mystic and proponent of Right Thinking, HT Hamblin, says: *...Indeed, lack of wholeness and completeness is foreign to the Mind of God...*

The Ideas in the Divine Mind are pristine and holy (whole) ~ they are not diminished or increased by our expression of them. Moreover they have a dynamic power and so it is said that when we 'touch' them they 'take us with them'. So, for instance, if we truly touch the spirit of Prosperity we will exude it in all we do ~ through positive and inspiring thoughts, through generous and timely acts. These Ideas are perfect, pure, inexhaustible, immutable and eternal. Moreover, they are reflected in the human soul and are its very fabric and the 'Stuff' out of which we create. By expressing them we celebrate the Divine Ideas in countless ways.

To plug into a real Idea is to plug into a great Power House. To align ourselves in this way with the Divine is to enter into a Prosperity which can never know the concept of lack. It is the 'Midas Consciousness' which reveals the 'Gold' in all things. This Consciousness allows us to see *through* people and events so we penetrate behind the sometimes ill-fitting outer garments ~ the awkward personality, idiosyncratic foibles, the apparent nature of circumstances ~ to the real person or meaning. This is to live in an altogether different, more enlightened, less judgemental way. It really only becomes possible to the degree that we move consciously closer to the Divine.

HT Hamblin points out the important fact that prosperity is based upon service. He says: *We should not think so much of 'What shall I get out of something?' as 'How helpful can I be?'* This truth is clearly timeless, for Hamblin's words in the early 20th Century are almost precisely those of Dr Wayne Dyer, the renowned 'New Age' writer and speaker in the 21st Century: *Ask not so much what I can get from a situation, but how may I serve?* Truth to tell, when we have love in our hearts, it is not at all hard to serve, and to fulfil wisely needs as they arise. As we move closer toward our infinite Source, so we find that we can draw upon that infinite supply.

Pause

Today, let's sip the nectar all around us and enjoy the prosperity consciousness.

The Joy of Giving and Receiving

God of time and eternity, whose Son reigns as servant, not master; we give you thanks and praise that you have blessed this Nation, The Realms and Territories with Elizabeth, our beloved and glorious Queen...

Excerpt from Special Prayer written at The Queen's direction by the Chapter of St Paul's Cathedral

One day at an auction I rescued a broken bust of Queen Victoria, modelled in parian. I have never had the bust professionally repaired, but daily it reminds me of Victoria's qualities ~ constancy, reliability and hard work. She celebrated her Diamond Jubilee in June 1897 with breakfast under the trees of Frogmore, near Windsor, where she laid her beloved husband, Prince Albert, to rest. Our own Queen celebrated her Diamond Jubilee in 2012 and this was marked by a Bank Holiday on the 5th of June, when celebrations took place throughout the UK and the Commonwealth. In 2012 every Commonwealth country was visited by at least one member of the Royal Family. Royalist or Republican, one cannot fail to be impressed by a Queen who despite her fair share of personal heartbreak, has borne with great patience and wisdom the responsibilities of reigning monarch. Never has she deviated in her resolve to serve or shown herself unwilling to carry the mantle of her office. Faith and prayer are, as she herself says, the bedrock of her life. How else could she carry such substantial responsibility? As Head of the Church of England, she is a committed Anglican and yet as Queen of the Commonwealth she recognises a broad spirituality. In one speech she said:

Whether we believe in God or not, I think most of us have a sense of the spiritual, that recognition of a deeper meaning and purpose in our lives, and

I believe that this sense flourishes despite the pressures of our world...This spirituality can be seen in the teachings of other great faiths. Of course religion can be divisive, but the Bible, the Koran and the sacred texts of the Jews and Hindus, Buddhists and Sikhs are all sources of divine inspiration and practical guidance passed down through the generations.

As many will know, there is a *Law of Reciprocal Service*. This can be represented pictorially as two interlaced circles. One represents giving and the other receiving. They are interlinked as giving and receiving cannot be divorced. The circle represents the continual giving and receiving of benefits ~ the bedrock upon which the whole fabric of society is founded. Invariably we find it easier to give than to receive, but receiving well is just as important as giving well. To give and receive well is to do so with wisdom and unconditionally, so we attach no conditions.

> ### *Pause*
>
> *Today, let's be fully present to how we are giving and receiving. Are we able to receive fully? Above all, can we give without expecting a return?*

Purity ~
Join Me in a Spiritual Shower...

Many years ago a soap manufacturer employed market researchers to go into schools in Kent to test a new range of skincare products. The children were asked a variety of questions and subsequently a soap was launched on to the mass market, which, contrary to the fashion of the time for highly coloured and fragrant soap, was devoid of colour and perfume. Subsequently a new soap was manufactured, called *Simple Soap,* which was the first of its type to be launched. One of the main attractions of this product (still going strong) is its purity, free from irritants and artificial colourants.

Throughout history the ideal of Purity has always had a deep and universal appeal. This is undoubtedly because it is of the very nature of the soul ~ pristine, unsullied, free from adulteration. Ideas too are pristine and pure, and to symbolise this Jakob Böhme, the great 16th Century mystic, rightly called them *beautiful virgins.*

As souls we always have choice, either to honour our precious, pristine nature by operating, as Jesus said: *In the world but not of it,* or to immerse ourselves in states of mind and actions which obscure our radiant beauty. But do we really want to live in a house with dirty windows where it is impossible to see out or to see in? This inevitably has a depressing effect, both upon ourselves and others. If we choose to wallow in a muddy bath, our light will undoubtedly be veiled, but once it is washed off our authentic nature can shine through again.

It is important to remember that no matter how ingrained is the darkness obscuring the light of the soul, it cannot penetrate her simple essence because that is pure spirit. This simple essence will always give the soul Herculean strength enough to free herself from the dark night of ignorance so that, once more, she can see the Light of Truth. To reveal herself to herself she must, metaphorically speaking, take a 'spiritual shower'. This consists of prayer, meditation, contemplation, worship and ritual which are like cleansing agents washing her clean. However, paradoxically, this cleansing must be done without touching the dirt. This is beautifully symbolised in one of the *Twelve Labours of Hercules* where Hercules (symbolising our souls) is asked to cleanse the Augean Stables which have not been cleansed for thirty years. Instead of doing this himself, Hercules delegates the work, diverting two rivers ~ Alpheus and Peneus ~ so that they flow through the stables and the work is accomplished. The secret of cleansing the dirt without touching it, is encapsulated in those famous words of Jesus about being *in* the world but not *of* it. This points to keeping ourselves pure by finding our Centre ~ the Spirit within ~ and *staying there*, whilst *at the same time* being fully present to each circumstance as it arises. We acknowledge our darkness and cleanse ourselves of it *without identifying with it*. The moment we identify ourselves with our problems we become lost and tend to lose perspective.

It helps to remember that we are each like Directors in the film set of our own lives. There may be lots of 'parts' but as Directors we must retain an overview of our lives. Thus, staying firmly in our Director's chair, we remain sensitive to all the 'parts' of ourselves (and the voices of others) but refrain from getting out of our chair to identify with any one of them. Then we remain safe and secure within our own centre, able to operate reasonably and calmly.

The *Twelve Labours of Hercules* explore the Path of the hero soul and the universal challenges which appear to all of us on our Journey from the many to the One and from the finite to the Infinite. Throughout our lives, the gauntlet is repeatedly thrown down. As each challenge arises, do we turn away or embrace it? In the face of these challenges, can we practise to remain perfectly centred? If we can do this, we can, figuratively speaking, 'keep our head when all about us are losing theirs'. We retain our essential purity by refusing to be persuaded or cajoled against our own better judgement.

Purity ~ Join Me in a Spiritual Shower...

Pause

Be still. Focus on the essential purity of your soul and the purity of thought and action that arises from it.

Is There a Plan for our Lives?

Getting into a car to share a trip out with a friend, we might say, *Well, what's the plan?* The friend may look at us blankly and retort, *There is no plan* or, *I was waiting for you so we could plan something together...* Whichever way we look at it, our lives are made up of plans. Many of these we decide for ourselves, some we decide with others and some are decided for us. If we are on holiday, we may tell ourselves that we are at leisure and decide not to make a plan as such. We may still enjoy our holiday but, without a knowledgeable guide to flag up things to do and see, we might miss a little piece of heaven on earth, or a significant site of some kind, that we later regret. And, of course, the consequences become more serious when we are urgently in need of something, but have no map to tell us where it is. So we can see that on a mundane level, maps and plans are essential to both the organisation of life and the full enjoyment of it. If this is true on a mundane level, how much more true must this be on a spiritual level. Although the path we walk will be as unique as we are, there are common themes and challenges which are well mapped. For instance, in John Bunyan's *Pilgrim's Progress,* Christian ~ representing the hero soul (you and me) ~ sets out from his hometown, the *City of Destruction* (the world and its ways) to the *Celestial City* (or Heaven). As he walks, he encounters all manner of challenges on his path. He is sent up blind alleys by well meaning, and not so well meaning, individuals. He encounters false teachers and people like 'Obstinate', 'Pliable' and 'Mistrust'. He enjoys the company of his friend, Faithful, but when he believes he has overtaken him, he suffers pride. He becomes familiar with the Slough of Despond and finds it difficult to extricate himself. The poem, *There's a Hole in my Sidewalk* by Portia Nelson, is another 'call to consciousness' used in more contemporary self-help literature. It is divided into five verses, as follows:

Is There a Plan for our Lives?

I walk down the street. There is a deep hole in the sidewalk. I fall in. I am lost. I am helpless. It isn't my fault. It takes forever to find a way out.

I walk down the same street. There is a deep hole in the sidewalk. I pretend I don't see it. I fall in again. I can't believe I am in this same place. But it isn't my fault. It still takes a long time to get out.

I walk down the same street. There is a deep hole in the sidewalk. I see it is there. I fall in... it's a habit... but my eyes are open. I know where I am. It is my fault. I get out immediately.

I walk down the same street. There is a deep hole in the sidewalk. I walk around it.

I walk down a different street.

The Twelve Labours of Hercules is another allegory which serves us extremely well as a map of the universal challenges we *all* face. Hercules is the hero soul who engages in twelve distinct labours. Once faced up to, and traversed, these free us from the bonds of ignorance and desire and allow us to gather our dissipated energies into one. Becoming one, we are able to see the Unity in all things. By reading and meditating on each challenge we can begin to see what is being asked of us *right now*.

Invariably our individual natures and circumstances become clear when projected against the backdrop of universal motifs and challenges which *all* souls are called to step up to at one time or another. So whilst the circumstances you and I contend with are unique, and in unique combinations, the archetypal challenges we *all* share. It is a journey well mapped.

Each Herculean task we undertake is more gripping than the most cutting edge drama, more real than the most moving play and more poignant than any 'story' one might see on cinema screen, YouTube or TV. We have the potential to live the Plan ~ as envisioned in the Divine Mind ~ *now*. The universal challenges depicted in great literature help us to see where we are going more clearly.

Whilst many of us recognise that there is a broad plan for our lives, we see that it is not a fatalistic one ~ we each have the free will to choose our path, to actualise our potentialities or not. How we get to our true Home is up to us, but we can be sure it is There ~ changeless, permanent and radiant.

Pause

Your true Home is within ~ return There as often as you can and be refreshed.

The Healing Balm of Forgiveness

Sitting in the 'Quiet Zone' on a train, the mobile phone of the man in front of me rang. He picked it up and started chatting. The person opposite got up. 'Excuse me,' he said, 'this is the Quiet Zone.' 'Oh I am sorry,' said the man, 'I hadn't realised.' 'That's OK,' said the stranger, 'I've done it myself.' The man smiled and retired to the connecting carriage.

In this small incident, forgiveness was present, both for the perpetrator, who said he was 'sorry' and smiled, and the injured party who not only accepted the apology but made the stranger feel less embarrassed by admitting that he too had done the same thing. This was a happy conclusion but, with the wrong attitude, it could so easily have been an unhappy one leading to anger and resentment.

From even a small incident like this, we can see that forgiveness cannot spread its healing balm until three things have happened:

- The recognition of a wrong done.
- A willingness to make reparation for it and to carry out that reparation.
- The acceptance by the injured party of that reparation.

This holds true for not only comparatively minor incidents, like the one on the train, but for serious incidents involving individuals, groups and even countries. Many of us remember the South African Reconciliation and Truth Commission which reported on murder, abduction and disappearances during the apartheid years. In the Report of the Commission, released in March 2003, is to be found a whole chapter of reparations. It is interesting to note that these reparations stretch across the whole gamut of South African society from the Business Sector and Civil Society, to what the witnesses had to say about reparation. Archbishop Desmond Tutu, who won the 1984 Nobel Peace Prize for his struggle against apartheid, and who chaired the Commission, said: *It has been an incredible privilege for those of us who served on the Commission to preside over the process of healing a traumatized and wounded people. We are also deeply grateful to the thousands of South Africans who came to the Commission to tell us their stories. They have won our country the admiration of the world: wherever one goes, South Africa's peaceful transition to democracy, culminating in the Truth and Reconciliation process, is spoken of almost in reverent tones, as a phenomenon that is unique for humankind. Other countries have had truth commissions and many more are following our example, but ours is regarded as the most ambitious, a kind of benchmark against which the rest are measured.*

Where there are weighty cases such as this and more ordinary cases, such as acrimonious divorce, highly trained and skilled mediators can turn the tide and bring order out of chaos. When conflict arises on a national scale, souls with particular and special gifts are required to bridge the gaps and facilitate the healing. (I imagine that the huge 'presence' and gravitas of Archbishop Desmond Tutu was such that perpetrators and injured were able to face each other and look each other in the eye.)

Turning now to the three things we need for forgiveness to take place. The first is recognition of a wrong done. If we are unaware that we have done wrong, there can be no progress. Where there is a serious wrong, there is an obligation to bring it to the perpetrator's attention. However, as seen in the train incident, it is *how* we do this that is important. Undoubtedly this takes great courage because, on the whole, it is easier and demands less of us, to 'leave things be'. However, when the incident is a minor one, it is equally true to say that if the loss to us in highlighting the truth to another is going to be greater than the gain to them, it may be right for us to remain silent, at least for the time being. As to major incidents, we will undoubtedly experience fear (as do most whistle blowers) but in the end we are bidden by our conscience to speak up.

On the second point, it seems to me that willingness to make reparation, and to carry it out, cannot be overlooked. In certain cases this may mean that one can do no more than say 'sorry' but in others this can be backed up by practical action of some kind. Reparation means that we have really accepted that we have done something wrong. In 1989 ninety-six football fans died when they were crushed during a game at the Hillsborough Stadium in Sheffield. On 12 September 2012 the Hillsborough Independent Panel disaster report was published. This revealed that 41 of the 96 victims had the potential to survive. It also found that South Yorkshire Police and emergency services attempted to deflect the blame for the crush onto the victims. The Football Association apologised unreservedly and David Cameron spoke for the whole government when he said that he was 'profoundly sorry'. Writing online for 'Cause4 Opinion' on 14 September, Nick Gandon wrote: *There is a golden opportunity for organisations, such as the Football Association, to humbly and in penitence, develop and fund new activities that will serve the people of Liverpool and its footballing communities; ones that will inspire and develop young people through football and demonstrate the transformational possibilities that sport ~ and education through sport ~ can palpably achieve.*

As to the *acceptance* of an apology and the capacity of the recipient to forgive an injustice, this is complex. Once the perpetrator recognises an injustice, it may be that he or she cannot experience real healing until they have been forgiven. We may be anxious for forgiveness for our own peace of mind. However, if it becomes evident that the injured party is not able to forgive, we may need to put this need to one side and offer up a prayer for self-forgiveness. Invariably, even when we are forgiven by others, self-forgiveness can take months or years.

> ### Pause
>
> When we do something we know is wrong, let's make whatever reparation we can. If we don't know how, let's ask for help from our guardian angel.
>
>

The Second Birth

It was that great soul, Socrates, who suggested that the soul takes great delight in new life as it serves to remind us of eternity which is forever young. Of course we all experienced a physical birth and live (on one level) a physical life, but there is another kind of birth ~ the so-called 'second birth'. This is the awakening of the soul to its innate divinity. With this second birth come new vehicles for expression as we become more conscious, more loving and more giving. It was the Master Jesus who said: *And no man putteth new wine into old bottles else the new wine doth burst the bottles and the wine is spilled and the bottles will be marred*: but the new wine must be put into new bottles.

By many, the end of the Mayan Calendar in 2012 was seen as the end of a cycle and the beginning of a new one. Many civilisations have recognised Great Ages or cycles of time. The Greeks recognised Golden, Silver, Bronze and Iron Ages. The Hindus too recognise equivalent periods of time called 'Yugas'. Each can be seen as an unfolding of consciousness. Whilst we are said to be living currently in the Kali Yuga (the Iron Age), where there is an inordinate focus on material goods, leading to materialism and multiplicity, it is possible to be living the Golden Age from within. In truth, we do this whenever we are engaged in spiritual study or prayer. These are cathartic, or cleansing, and serve to 'slough off' the materialism of our Age.

When a transition from one state to another, or one age to another, is about to take place, there are signs of unrest. The 'clothes' that once fitted so well no longer fit and we begin to feel confined and unable to express ourselves freely. If this is true for the individual, it is true for society at large. It therefore becomes imperative that we find new vehicles for the expression of life. Whether we are talking about individuals or larger groups and countries, if we cannot find new vehicles for expression our gifts atrophy and we become stale and cease to feel truly alive.

As new ideas 'push' to be born and new life seeks to find a way through, there is invariably a corresponding backlash from elements within ourselves and within society which are belligerent and darned if they will change! The more threatened we feel by change, the greater will be the wall we build to hide behind. Many of us recognise that this stems from fear. A movement back to what is known is the equivalent of trying to put new wine into old sacks. No matter how much we try to push our new ideas into safe and well-trodden avenues, as any child knows, it will not work! Just remember the frustration generated when, as toddlers, we attempted to force plastic shapes into a space which didn't fit!

We can see how organisations, societies and whole countries become unable to move forward because of the stranglehold of outmoded dogmas. Some regimes may use brute force to impose ideas on their peoples despite domestic and international condemnation. As a result, bodies like the UN and organisations like Amnesty International have grown up to defend people's rights. We, too, can make a tremendous difference by supporting organisations promoting the welfare of all. We can also make our presence count through online bodies, like Avaaz ~ a community-based campaigning organisation. But most of all, by following our Star ~ our spiritual path, we can help raise humankind.

There are some shining stars ~ 'shooting stars' ~ who, through their courageous thoughts and acts, have lit up the night sky and brought new life. Their wish is always to embrace timeless truths and 'find a better way'. Fortunately, there are many shining stars, but two comparatively recent ones are climate activists and campaigners: Polly Higgins, a lawyer, who passed away, aged just 50, in 2019 and teenager, Greta Thunberg, a Swedish schoolgirl. Polly worked hard to create a law to criminalise ecological damage and in the process even sold her home and gave up her job. Her work continues through others. Greta began her days by standing outside the Swedish parliament, holding up a sign saying, 'School Strike for Climate' and went on to spread the word across the world. She advocates peaceful civil disobedience.

We can each light up the night sky because we all come from the same Divine Source. May new life be ours as we awaken to the reality of the Truth that does not change.

Pause

Today, 'Be the change you want to see in the world.'

Mohandas Gandhi

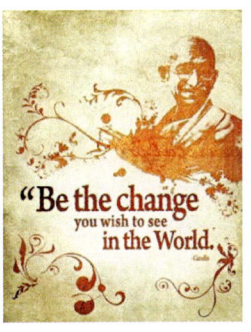

Journey to the Centre of Ourselves

The closer we come to the centre of anything ~ be it a person, a family or an organisation ~ the more clearly we see. If that is true for all these, it is certainly true of ourselves! It is worth reflecting that if the Divine is at the centre of all things, then when we approach the centre of anything we come close to that One ~ the Centre in which all centres are rooted. This can be mystically understood by remembering that God is an infinite sphere, whose centre is everywhere and whose circumference is nowhere. [1]

Drawing inwards to our own centre, we become still and calm, less agitated by the winds of change, less moved by others' opinions and more moved by our own inner wisdom. This puts me in mind of a friend, Jennifer Dunkley, who recounts a meditation where students were asked to imagine themselves rotating on the outer edge of a giant gramophone record. The record spins at great speed and they become quite giddy. However, when they draw to the centre of the record, what a difference... the movement becomes slower and they can enjoy the scenery. It seems that that centre is a good 'place' to be!

So it is that when we draw to the centre of ourselves, life takes on a whole new perspective. We become fully focussed, dynamic and powerful ~ our often dissipated energies are drawn into a unity and consequently we can see clearly instead of in a desultory sort of way. It is as if we can view everything from atop the summit of a mountain rather than from the foothills. Life becomes more coherent and we begin to see and hear more clearly. We find we can breathe freely and the myopic view from those foothills no longer throws us into confusion. Just take a moment to breathe in that pure mountain air and to be...

This mountain view liberates us from the multitude of 'needs' and 'wants' which grow up apace in the lowlands, very much like the head of the Hydra in Greek mythology which gave rise to two new heads each time one was severed. Instead, there is the possibility for our energies to become unified, focussed and very powerful. Gradually, as our faculties open like the lotus blossom, we begin to see the world through the Eye of That within us which is God. Just try now to imagine how the world might look... In that Divine Vision there is no separateness. Everything is unique, beautiful and true. In fact the word 'cosmos' means, 'beautiful order'. There is complete harmony as all the parts stand in perfect relationship to each other and the whole from which they come. Manyness proceeds from Unity and celebrates Unity. For instance, a single fertilized egg produces all the cells, organs and tissues that make up our bodies. Trees are many but have been found to have mycorrhizal fungal networks which mean they can communicate with each other and live as one community.

In the Divine Vision there is no distinction between the Knower and the Known and the Knowing which links them. When we are inspired, we too are lifted up into that unific Vision.

Coming to our own centre, we are immediately brought into relationship with all beings who, like us, have their centres in that Great Centre wherein is rooted all that is. This is inspiring! This is why Jesus encourages us to 'Seek first the Kingdom of God and all things will be added.' In other words, if we find the Centre (the Kingdom) in ourselves, we find all things 'There' with us. To find the Centre is to know ourselves and to know all beings and all things in ourselves.

The more we become truly who we are, the greater the opportunities presented to us and the more able we are to fulfil them and so have a leavening effect on the world. As we work with others, in the true spirit of the Aquarian Age, we begin to appreciate the unique gifts we each have to offer. This ignites ~ literally sets us on fire ~ with the spirit of service without which no society can prosper. We learn to value each other, putting away that false spirit of individualism and obstinacy ('my way is the right way') which Aquarius symbolises in its more negatives phases.

The Colours of Virtue

We need to be wide awake and intensely alert in order to resist the sleep-inducing influences of worldly attraction. In our own century this is even more imperative as there is greater and more diverse materialism to engage us and draw us into the sleep state. In a sense, materialism, in all its forms, is the drug that induces sleep. In the journey to the centre of ourselves, it is vital that we work in the clear light of day for only then will the shadows recede and Reality be revealed.

[1] Attributed to Hermes Trismegistus

Pause

Drawing inwards to our Centre, we become still and calm, less agitated by the winds of change, less moved by others' opinions and more moved by our own inner wisdom.

WISDOM

Follow the Pilot

Fish have the freedom of water, birds have the freedom of the air, animals have the freedom of the Earth, but as humans we not only have all of these, we have the unique privilege of enjoying the freedom of fire ~ the domain of creative thought, imagination and intuition.

I stepped into the Easyjet Airbus at Gatwick anticipating a fabulous view of land, sea and mountains, but alas the clouds obscured my vision. Life is so often like that. We cannot enjoy the freedom of the moment because we are preoccupied with our own concerns and anxieties ~ the clouds that hover in our lives. On my journey it seemed to me that the clouds symbolised my ignorance and it became clear that our views are inevitably obscured by the degree of our ignorance. It is ignorance that darkens our vision of real being and keeps us from being truly free. It also prevents us from stepping-up into the freedom of our inheritance, for made in the image of the Divine, we were born free! It is our 'sleep and forgetting', and the poor choices which flow from that, which limit our freedom. How to break through to the blue sky of Truth?

As the airbus ascended from the runway my view expanded and I realised that the earth-bound view, that we invariably accept as normal, is pitifully inadequate. So often we assume that what is apparent to us at any one time is the whole Truth, when really we have hardly got off the ground! The 'Pilot' knows otherwise. Unlike the passenger, he understands that in order to arrive at his destination or Goal, he must first know the direction in which to travel and conscientiously, despite the onslaught of poor weather conditions (states of mind), keep the nose of his plane firmly focussed on its destination. He knows that if he desists, even momentarily, his plane could spin out of control. He must keep to the direction of his target no matter what.

The Pilot enjoys the freedom of the airspace but in order to make the journey as comfortable as possible for the passengers, he must only gradually increase the height at which he is flying. If he does this too quickly his passengers will be thrown in all directions. The journey into Truth is so often a gradual ascent although sudden 'spurts' of growth are not precluded. The words of Tibetan monk, Dr Akong Tulku, are illuminating when it comes to gradual unfolding. He says: *This searching for freedom too soon is like house martins jumping out of their nest too early and then crashing to the ground. Such situations are commonplace and generally accepted as normal, but in many cases children can end up in institutions simply because they have too much freedom too soon.*

As the Pilot ascends he invariably enters periods of intense turbulence where he is called upon to use all his resolve and strength to keep his plane on course. This turbulence, representing life's challenges, comes to test the depth and breadth of our resolve. Sometimes we are shaken up so badly that we lose our perspective and plummet to the 'downstairs' view with its inevitable 'half-tied' vision of things. The Pilot sees our distress and our flailing about and feels immense compassion. However, he presses on regardless. Invariably, though, we are so caught up in the stresses and strains of everyday living that we pay very little attention to the Pilot and consequently we lose sight of our destination. This is when we are least free.

Come rain or shine the plane ascends, even imperceptibly and, as it does so, our view expands, encompassing greater and more splendid vistas, but such is our habit, we may fail to look out of the window! Did we but know it ~ we are now flying above the clouds and turbulence has ceased. The Pilot tries to tell us that, having risen above the clouds, fair weather is the order of the day, but are we listening? Now, having reached the greatest height, there is a freedom and a vision we have not experienced before. One day we reach our destination. The Sun is there to greet us as we step into Its embrace. No longer do we 'See through a glass darkly; but face to face.' [1]

---

[1] Corinthians 13:12

Pause

Rising above the clouds, fair weather is the order of the day. Let's be directed by our inner Pilot.

The Law of Reciprocal Service

A life without gratitude seems hardly conceivable and yet it is possible to live for a time in the dark.

From an early age, the importance of saying 'please' and 'thank you' was impressed upon us by our parents and teachers. Essentially this represents a coming of age as when we were very young we were dominated by our appetites and took whatever was offered to us without a second thought.

As we get older, and with the help of our parents, we begin consciously to appreciate what we receive and express this in words and good manners. It is true to say that as we grow in love and become more aware, our sense of appreciation grows and we come to more fully appreciate the true spirit of giving and receiving.

Again, some of us were fortunate in being taught early on that the food on our plates and the water from the tap came not just from the Earth but from the Divine. If we were very fortunate, we were encouraged to express our gratitude through a short prayer before eating and perhaps also before sleeping, when we 'climbed the wooden hill' to bed. All these things served to instil a sense of gratitude which, hopefully, we have taken with us into life.

On the other hand, we may not have appreciated life's bounty. As a child I distinctly recall the daily school assembly where Mr Hoskins, the Deputy Head, would encourage us to thank God for the gifts we enjoyed, things like sight and hearing. At the time I did not pay much attention to these homilies. These things seemed so much part of me, I hardly gave them

The Law of Reciprocal Service

another thought. It wasn't until much later that I appreciated that sight and sound ~ like the very air we breathe ~ are gifts from the Divine. Clearly they far outweigh any material gift.

Much later, I came to appreciate that true gratitude could only flower when I moved from 'me' and 'mine' to 'you' and 'yours', then to 'ours' and ultimately to the Divine. This seems to show that as we grow in maturity our consciousness expands, moving out from the centre of ourselves to embrace more and more ~ parents, siblings, family, friends, colleagues, relationships with local community and worldwide community, whether through travel or the worldwide web. Overarching and yet at the same time substanding these relationships, is the Providential energy flowing from that Great One which mysteriously links one thing to another and maximises every opportunity to create further good.

As we grow, our sense of gratitude deepens and we begin to see that the Divine is the greatest Giver and, indeed, the Supreme Receiver. This Giving and Receiving is perfect in the sense that our Source not only 'knows' *what* to give, but *how* to give and *when* to give. This is the Model for our way of living.

Gratitude flowers when we become conscious of the degree to which we are receiving, every minute of every day. The opposite occurs when we are ungrateful ~ when there is no appreciation of having received anything at all. This inevitably leads to a sense of isolation and a feeling of entitlement, that the world somehow owes us a living. This is quite different from that spiritual state which gives freely and wisely, trusting in Providence.

Gratitude is born when we truly appreciate what we have received. The law of expression asks that we show that appreciation in some external form whether it be a 'thank you', a smile, a hug, a card, or in some other way. Giving and receiving are linked in a lifelong partnership. If we cannot give freely (unconditionally) we cannot receive freely either. Timing is important, as we may be given something at a stage when we can't possibly be expected to appreciate it. Educators know this, as children must first learn A, B, C before they can form words and begin to write, and retailers clearly label games as only suitable for children of certain ages. To give unwisely and indiscriminately is to invite indifference and misuse of what has been given. To give unwisely can also mean that the loss to us is greater than the benefit received by the other person or organisation.

Mostly we are grateful when we receive just what we need at any given time. In this sense the onus is on the giver to determine what might be needed, and to administer it wisely, and on the receiver to be open about what is really needed. Sometimes we don't get it right! However, most of us comprehend the spirit behind the giving, so we can express gratitude even when we are disappointed.

It is hard enough to know the needs of the people closest to us, and yet world leaders must consider the needs of whole societies and nations. And yet... there are needs that are common to us all ~ the need for food, water and shelter and then the need for family, community, education and spiritual nourishment. We are fortunate as many of us enjoy all, or most, of these ~ sometimes to the point where we take them for granted. That's why it's important to become aware of them and relish them on a daily basis because only then can we be truly thankful.

Pause

Can we give freely today ~ not looking for a 'return' of some kind? Can we also receive freely without feeling unworthy of the gift?

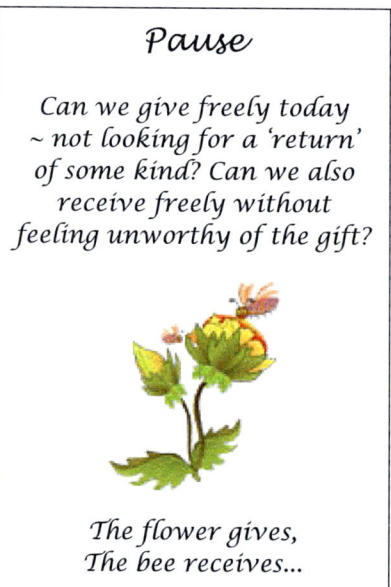

*The flower gives,
The bee receives...*

Courageous Living Always Speaks to Us

In April 2014, mulling over the theme of this vignette ~ Living Courageously ~ it struck me that it was actually St George's Day. How appropriate, I thought. By 'chance' I began the day at a St George's Day Parade in the picturesque old fishing village of Emsworth, just a few miles from Bosham in West Sussex. This day marked the departure of troops from the 47th Royal Artillery Regiment, who had been based at Baker Barracks, Thorney Island, for 25 years. There was a stirring parade through the village and TV cameras and reporters recorded the proceedings. The Regiment was sad to leave but hoped to retain links with the area. The 12th Regiment Royal Artillery are now at Baker Barracks.

Being on parade so to speak, I felt it might be helpful to approach the men and women of the 47th Regiment to ask them what they felt about Courage. My first encounter was with a female Lance Bombadier. She felt there were two types of Courage: moral and physical. Moral courage she described as doing something we believe in and sticking to our 'moral guns', even when others think otherwise. Moreover, she felt that Courage did not mean not feeling fear, but rather that we elect to overcome it. This conversation seemed like an auspicious start in my quest to penetrate to the heart of Courage. I therefore moved on to speak to the men of the Regiment, but I did not receive the response I expected! When I framed my question all but one of the soldiers disappeared. He suggested I spoke to the elderly military veterans seated in the Market Square.

There are many men and women who live life courageously but prefer not to talk about it. One such person is Sophie Christiansen. Sophie was born in 1987 two months premature. She has cerebral palsy and at age six began horse riding as a form of physiotherapy. Despite, or perhaps because of, her disabilities, she excelled at horse riding and particularly dressage. To date she has won many medals including three Gold Medals in the Paralympic Games and in 2013 she was awarded an OBE for her services to equestrianism. We can all cite examples of beautiful souls, like Sophie, who are courageous in their thoughts and actions, but what is the essential nature of Courage? My trusty Webster's dictionary suggests that it involves heart, mind and will and certainly Ideal Courage would draw upon all three. We can also think about Courage as the virtue of fortitude. All hero souls possess fortitude and live full and fruitful lives despite deformity, sickness and deprivation. Virtues are said to be 'excellences' of the soul. Invariably we only see them in others or know them in ourselves when difficult circumstances arise. They may fly in the face of conventional wisdom and what society deems to be 'right', but they bring us back to Truth and remind us of what is real. This is why the seeming fool can teach the apparently wise, as did the Fool to King Lear!

When we read about lives of courage, the spirit of courage awakens within us. When it is exercised, that spirit is fulfilled. We are stirred by stories of courage; fired up by courageous acts; humbled by those who, although far less well off or healthy than we are, yet live fuller and richer lives ~ lives which shine out and strengthen and give hope to all who witness them. Challenging circumstances are to be welcomed, and indeed embraced, because they represent golden opportunities for us to manifest God-like virtues. Sometimes in the quest for the essence of a quality or virtue it is helpful to imagine what life would be like without it. And so, just what would life be like without courage? Clearly the instinct of self-preservation would dominate so that we would be disinclined to really meet life, preferring to protect ourselves and withdraw. Opportunities which daily present themselves to help us grow would be eschewed as threats to our creature comforts. Let us all keep facing the challenges of life, grasping those prickly nettles and finding the courage within to step up and expand our horizons within and without.

Pause

Let's step up and expand our horizons with courage and confidence.

The Wisdom of the Sunflower

Some months ago I was given a present ~ a tiny sapling in a flowerpot. I was told it was a sunflower. It looked vulnerable and I decided to plant and water it pretty much straightaway. At first it seemed undecided as to whether it wanted to survive, seeming to turn yellow in parts and keel over! However, as I consistently watered it, it became stronger and began to shoot up ~ gradually at first and then faster and faster until now, in August, it has reached a great height. This flower has a majesty and dignity about it that we can all recognise. Its sweet yellow head has opened fully and it spends every moment adoring its namesake, the Sun. Like all nature, the Sunflower has its own innate wisdom. We can learn from it how to nourish ourselves. Come rain or shine, it always follows the Sun from east to west, making a complete circuit each day. We don't need a sundial or a watch if we can learn to tell the time by the Sunflower!

We can imitate the Sunflower by following the Sun, the Divine Spark within. If we can do this as consistently as the Sunflower, everything we bring to life will be timely. By putting the Divine Sun at the centre of our lives we have no need to 'seek what to eat or what to drink or to be of anxious mind'. Once we learn the wisdom of the Sunflower we shall never again turn our back on the Sun but always face It and be illumined and warmed by It. And we can be healed by the Sun on a physical level too. After a cold winter, very few of us are not restored by the touch of warm Spring sunshine on our cheeks. And even in winter, the Sun has a great power to heal and uplift. Just recently I walked out on a cold and frosty morning and became transfixed at the sight of the Sun's rays streaming through a hedge in someone's garden, close to a nearby field. So beautiful was the vision that I went to stand in those rays and felt myself healed by them. When we align ourselves to the Sun, turning our faces towards it, we put ourselves in a position to receive its life-giving properties. It is a deep truth that we cannot receive fully until we become like the object of our worship. The Sunflower not only opens fully to the Sun, it is in many respects like it. It was the Greek philosopher Plotinus who summed this up well in the words: ... *Remember above all that as the eye could not behold the Sun unless it were Sunlike itself, so the soul can only see Beauty by becoming Beautiful herself.*

By turning to the Sun, everything in our lives comes into alignment and everything is nourished. The 20th century thinker and writer Henry Thomas Hamblin wrote a book called *Divine Adjustment*. In the preface he says: *There is an ever-present Principle of Perfection which, when co-operated with, brings our own personal life into a state of order.* As we come to know the Divine Sun in our depths, every detail of our lives falls into place and therefore there is no need to become involved in minutiae (in today's terms, what might be called 'not sweating the small stuff'). Hamblin discovered the importance of 'right valuation' early in life when he became absorbed by the question of diet, proselytising a rigid regime of fasting, eating fruit and nuts and exercising. His weight dropped rapidly from twelve to nine stone and he suffered frequent colds. It was some time later that he realised he had 'put the cart before the horse' and that as his preoccupation with external nourishment (ie diet) had grown, his concentration on inner nourishment had diminished.

As many of us appreciate, spiritual reading is a primary source of nourishment. Spiritual classics like the Bible, *Tao Teh Ching* and *Bhagavad Gita* are, in particular, endless sources of wisdom, as is the inspiring prose and poetry of more contemporary authors. We can return to our favourite books again and again, memorise favourite lines and draw sustenance from them.

The Sunflower assiduously, and yet without effort, follows the Sun. Can we do the same?

Pause

Today, let's try to launch each new activity with a pure intention and so align ourselves to the Sun.

A Winter's Retreat

This morning I invite you to a Winter's retreat in a Guest House penned by the poet Rumi... so make yourself a warm drink, draw up a comfortable chair, wrap yourself up in a warm blanket and settle down. Rumi writes:

This being human is a guest house,
Every morning a new arrival.
A joy, a depression, a meanness,
some momentary awareness comes as an unexpected visitor.
... Be grateful for whoever comes,
because each has been sent
as a guide from beyond.

> ### *Pause*
>
> *Who, or what, will be your 'new arrival' today? Teachers may come in disguise. Can you embrace whatever comes?*
>
>

HOSPITALITY

Lark Ascending

Visiting a local nursing home recently I noticed a cockatiel ~ a pretty bird with distinctive grey and yellow face and rouge cheeks ~ perched in a cage. Whenever I see a creature caged, a feeling of sadness arises within me. This time I decided to stay with that feeling and explore it. After a while I realised that the sadness surfaces whenever I see something prevented from fulfilling its purpose. In the case of a bird, it is very clear that its nature is to fly. In fact we could say that its reason for being ~ its raison d'être ~ is to fly. We have all watched birds dip and soar, sometimes dancing together in astounding swirling patterns where the many become one. The joy they experience is almost palpable as we watch them delight in the freedom of the skies and, mysteriously, that same joy and freedom is communicated to us as we witness their dance ~ a joy captured in many art forms by artists, poets and indeed composers. Once heard, Vaughan Williams' *The Lark Ascending* can never be forgotten and it makes the heart sing!

We too can experience the freedom of the aerial kingdom as, like birds, our thoughts are winged; through them we can rise above the limitations of our bodies and personalities and break through the clouds into the clear light of Day where Truth resides. Finding this, who wouldn't want to sing as sweetly as any bird... And that is the other raison d'être of the bird ~ the ability to sing, not for any reason but out of sheer joy. There is nothing so poignant, so beautiful and yet so tragic, as to hear a caged bird sing. 'Beautiful' because a bird will sing almost regardless of its conditions, 'tragic' because it sings in an environment for which it was not made, an environment which stifles its nature and purpose.

Men and women too have sung in cages which are equally hostile, and yet for all that, they have sung most sweetly... Nelson Mandela was imprisoned for twenty -seven years on Robben Island; Terry Waite was imprisoned for five years as a captive in Lebanon; the Catholic missionary, Fr. Paul McAuley, who, despite considerable risk to his personal safety, remained in Peru and subsequently died there in the spring of 2019. And there are others too who, out of compassion, have elected to sing in cages. One such beautiful soul is the Belgian, Father Damien, (now Saint Damien) who quarantined himself on the Island of Molokai to care for the lepers there and then died alongside those to whom he ministered.

It is the understanding of a thing's purpose, and its freedom to fulfil that purpose, which allows it to live fully and that is true for us too. Since all things are connected in the Great Chain of Being, that purpose is a collective one as well as an individual one. What we achieve, we achieve for the whole of humanity and creation; what we fail to achieve, we equally fail to achieve for all. As the 20th century thinker and writer, HT Hamblin, so cogently points out, we must stop dwelling on our shortcomings and compounding those by repeating them to friends and family, because ...*this is only a recital of our falling short of that which is true, and is not a recital of that which is true*. If we can but remember (and grow in the understanding of) the glorious measure of Man... *For Thou hast made him a little lower than the angels and hast crowned him with glory and honour.* (Psalm 8, v.5).

In the same way that we ponder the purpose of a bird or anything else, we can reflect on our purpose. With the creatures of nature we share five senses; we also share instincts like self-preservation and self-expression and the need for companionship with our own kind. However, unlike these creatures we can think self-consciously, we can say 'I'. It is Reason and Intuition which make us distinctly human and allow us to survey the interior world and come closer to our Source. If we fail to use these higher faculties, we can continue to enjoy our lives on a natural level, but we fall short of being truly human, realising but a small part of our potential. The 'many mansions' of which Jesus spoke are left unexplored. It is the truth of our own nature that will set us free. We each have a key to unlock the door, but freedom is only possible when we know who we are ('Man Know Thyself') and how to exercise our latent potentialities. This is why a spiritual education is so important. Until we know something of our purpose, we remain trapped in our own self-built cages. Today is the day... the day when we can choose to find out the truth about ourselves and our God-given purpose.

> *Pause*
>
> *Today is the day... the day when we can be 'larks ascending' ~ finding out the truth about ourselves and our purpose.*
>
>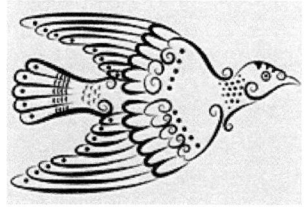

All Pervading Light

I would like to invite you to celebrate Light with me. Every day we take it for granted that the Sun will rise in the East and set in the West. It is such a constant in our lives that we forget to be aware of it and indeed to give thanks for it. Light is not only external, it lives within us. We honour the light in everything and everyone when we recognise it consciously and give expression to it in some form. This can be by gently smelling the fragrance of a rose, being aware of the rich perfume and peaty smell of the earth after it has rained, or it can be by shaking someone's hand or kissing them in greeting or by putting our hands together and affirming out loud or silently, 'The light in me bows to the light in you'. Light is omnipresent and a wonderful symbol of Divine Truth as no dark corner can escape it. By honouring the Light we see the Divine in all things and all things in the Divine.

2015 was the International Year of Light. It is still hard to believe that children in Asia and Africa often have no option but to live and study by the light of a naked flame. Being alive to Light makes us aware that so often we take artificial light for granted, but in many parts of the world there is little to light the dark evenings, or it comes at an immense cost, as the burning of kerosene lamps (sometimes crudely fashioned from old food cans) contributes greatly to global warming.

Many years ago now I visited the National Gallery and saw an exhibition of paintings by the artist Camille Pissarro. Like many of the Impressionist painters, he was interested in the effects of light. In order to explore this he painted the same scene at different times of day and at night. The scene remained largely unchanged, but the various hues of light had the effect of casting emphases on this or that figure, bringing a clarity or obscurity that had not been there before. The paintings depict the same scene but are very different. Of course all painters are aware of the play of light, but using the same scene and painting it at different times serves to demonstrate just how important light is in terms of introducing atmosphere and transforming people and objects. We only have to think of the Transfiguration of Jesus to recall how the Divine Light *made his raiment shining, exceeding white as snow... and his face shone like the sun.*

We can use a whole dictionary of terms to celebrate the nuances of light: dappled, lustrous, shining, radiant, flashing, lucid, luminous, luminescent, opaque, penumbral (partially shaded), resplendent, spectral, shimmering, translucent.

As souls we shine by the Light of the Spirit within ~ the one Light which binds and embraces us all. And yet... as unique souls we shine in our own distinctive way, casting Light on particular aspects of creation ~ some of us serve by shining Light on the kingdoms of nature; others shine Light on the various human sciences and arts, yet others shine Light on the Divine through their interest in Ideal Philosophy, Religion and Mysticism. As we shine our Light, so we highlight some particular aspect of Reality and in so doing raise its profile. This is akin to a common experience ~ that of sharing... When out walking we see something we enjoy, we invariably point it out to our companions, summoning it from background to foreground so that they too can share the moment and enjoy it with us. Depending upon how many friends we share the moment with, the celebration is multiplied by that number because each will see the same thing from a slightly different angle.

It was Jesus who said, *Let your light so shine before men, that they may see your good works, and glorify your Father which is in heaven.* Let us make our being in the world count ~ let the Light ~ let our Light shine!

Pause

Let's not be shy in coming forward but sound our own note confidently.

Present and Connected

From cradle to grave we are linked to the Earth, to every kingdom of nature and to each other by innumerable ties. Some of these are so obvious as to hardly need mentioning whilst others are more subtle, revealing themselves only to the consciousness which has unfolded to meet them. This is based on the premise that like is really only knowable to like, so inevitably we pass over those things we are not yet able to see. For instance, the eye of a trained artist will pick up a whole gamut of meaning in a painting that you and I would miss. From experience, we all know that study in any field will necessarily bring to light a host of aspects which were hidden to us before. As we unfold our understanding and adopt an open attitude ~ what mindfulness teachers call 'Friendly Curiosity' ~ the incidence of synchronicity seems to increase. This is because we slow down enough to notice all sorts of connections we might otherwise have passed over.

Synchronicity can be defined as a meaningful tie-up between an inner psychic state and an outward manifestation or event. So when we are intently focussed on something, whether it be exploring an idea, writing a letter or completing a task of some kind, that focus will act as a magnet attracting experiences and people into our lives who can offer valuable insights, enriching our task and bringing it closer to completion.

Ideas themselves have tremendous attracting power connecting both people and insights. It is as if each idea we hold constellates around it ideas, events and people of a like nature. Ideas manifest in actions and shape our lives. That is why the ancients told us to be careful about what we think because thoughts become actions and actions give rise to our environment. Real Ideas are timeless, eternal and infinite. Each is like a pure stream, rooted in the Ocean, with small rivulets flowing constantly from and to it. The more universal the Idea, the more dynamic it is and the more it stands as parent to the family of ideas it gives rise to and embraces. Hence, the absolutely universal Ideas of Unity, Goodness, Truth and Beauty contain within them, and have flowing from them, a veritable brood of unities, goodnesses, truths and beauties, all manifesting in different ways in a vast connected web. Whenever we fall silent and ponder, we can witness this family of connections and gradually come to see the whole manifested world as one vast symbol of the Ideas of which it is a mirror.

We can all experience the power of the cathartic arts (spiritual reading, prayer, meditation, contemplation, ritual) to bring us closer to our Centre ~ the summit from which to view the huge tapestry of connections all around us. When we are off centre, or out of sorts, the life-giving world of connections closes down to us ~ we feel outside 'the flow', stranded, separate, miserable. This is anathema to the spirit in each one of us which is always present and connected. When we are 'in the flow' again, we become awake once more to the many nuances of life ~ the 'black' and 'white' of separation turns into the whole gamut of colour, representing connection and relationship.

It is then that we become aware of synchronicities ~ unexpected meetings, a word, a gesture, a passage from a book, which serve to nourish us and bring us closer to our goals. We realise then that the universe is benevolent ~ that Providence is reliable and will *always* bring about the connections that need to be made.

The Swiss psychologist Carl Jung coined the term *Synchronicity*, describing it as an 'Acausal Connecting Principle' where events and circumstances are not causally linked but nonetheless converge to reveal a universe throbbing with meaning, affinity and relationship.

The idea of connection is also revealed in quantum physics where, regardless of distance, entangled particles remain connected so that actions performed on one particle affect the other. We are all connected. What I do affects you and what you do affects me and this increases in proportion to our closeness.

The Great Connector is of course Love. It is Love that connects the Lover to the Beloved. The Ladder of Love in Plato's *Symposium* is relevant, each step representing a different manifestation of love, from the lower more physical rungs to the highest, representing the love of Beauty Itself (as opposed to beautiful things which are beautiful because they participate in Beauty).

When we become connected through love there is huge potential to harness joint energies and so change the world for the good. Most importantly we can begin to be like Love itself ~ a bridge ~ creatively linking insights, events and people.

Pause

Can you remain 'present' and connected throughout the day, creating bridges as you go?

Listening to the Still Small Voice

Boarding the 700 bus which runs along the South Coast to Brighton, I couldn't help but reflect on the sound system ~ 'Pottery Lane', 'The Barleycorn', 'Drift Lane', the voice blurted out. The message matches up with the indicator board which repeats the words visually in bright orange. Of course this is particularly helpful to those whose sight or hearing may be compromised.

For some of us this 'age of the message' is not always helpful. We want to be able to hear the important ones, but so often we are subjected to a barrage of visual and audio messages which are superfluous. Instead of enjoying the silence, we must contend with repeated messages (such as the supermarket's, 'Would you like a bag?' and the 'travel speak' of public transport), plus the sound of mobile phones, loud conversations and music!

The increasing emphasis placed on peripheral and needless communication means that we can quite easily fail to hear the voice of our own guiding spirit or guardian angel. We are said to choose our guiding spirit and it remains with us throughout life, protectively watching over us. However, free will is sacrosanct and it will not intercede unless we ask for guidance. If there is one Voice we should be listening to, that is it! However, with the advent of more sophisticated technology and entertainment, the verbal and visual 'smog' has grown significantly ~ it tends to act as a distraction and we become reluctant to sit in the silence and wait for inner illumination. But when we do sit in the silence, we become nourished and supported by that Voice. We are shown a path through the densely populated 'wood' of the world and we draw to our centre. Striking a gong or ringing a bell can serve to remind us of our inner Voice and draw us back to our centre.

Again, listening to birdsong, the pounding of waves against the shore, the trickle of a stream, or any other sound of nature, has the capacity to bring us back to ourselves ~ to make us balanced again. Listen now... what can you hear? It could be a suggestion to reflect upon something; to read a text; to simply stay silent; to act upon something; to listen to someone. So often, when we listen to another's words, we are only half listening and consequently misunderstandings arise. If not that, then we silently anticipate an unfinished sentence or interject to complete it.

Quite possibly, the renaissance in 'mindfulness' over the last few years has come about through a beneficent guiding spirit and a collective understanding that we are out of balance. When the need for something arises, it attracts a response and the more urgent the need, the more cogent the response. Many acknowledge that the pace of life has increased, largely through technology, but also we have become disorientated by the emphasis on the physical plane ~ our senses dulled by 'reward points', the all year round 'sale' and 'experiences' for purchase on display stands. Quite simply, the Still Small Voice has been drowned out by the noise of 21st Century living. To hear it again, we must slow down and begin to notice what is around and within us, doing our best to be present fully to each person and situation. Everything we hear, see, touch, taste and smell with our senses is symbolic of something deeper. Instead of looking 'at' things, we can start to look 'through' them and so touch the stainless window of Eternity.

> *Pause*
>
> *Today can we listen and be present fully to each situation as it arises?*
>
>

Perfect Order all Around

The Vedic philosopher and writer, Ronald Lello, wrote: *...perception of the 'perfect' and the 'order' of creation is all to do with the way we are looking...* Without really looking, we can perceive no pattern, no order, just what appears to be a chaotic jumble. Indeed, this is the way some people see life. An apparently chaotic jumble was what I witnessed when I visited Truro Cathedral some years ago. Much of the south aisle was filled, knee deep, with what appeared to be mountains of screwed up newspaper! I found it visually offensive and my line of thought went a bit like this... 'Oh no, what a dreadful prospect in such a beautiful setting'... followed quickly by: 'Not another "statement"...' I'm tired of these visual gimmicks, let's have some real art that will uplift and inspire.' Immediately, the alarm bells sounded and I knew I was reacting without looking properly. Time to centre myself and find out more... I approached a young woman standing nearby who explained more about the artist and the reason for his creation ~ what appeared to be a meaningless jumble of paper suddenly became meaningful. It then struck me that things become meaningful when we see the pattern or order behind them ~ their reason for being.

The creator of this art installation was Imran Qureshi, an artist from Lahore. The piece is called, 'After which I am no more I and you are no more you'. It was constructed of 30,000 sheets of paper. In fact, it is not newspaper as I first thought, but a torn up printed photo of a vast floor painting of green foliage. Qureshi uses this to highlight the idea of 'garden' as portrayed in the Bible, the Qur'an and other holy books. The pile of paper is also designed to signify the idea of 'mountain', but its overriding message is powerful... From a distance, the crumpled paper symbolises the way in which we tend to look at groups of people from afar, like refugees for instance. Invariably we see them as faceless bodies, somehow separate from us. Often, we 'brand' or homogenise people in this way. We lose sight of who they are. However, if we walk up close to the paper, we see something rather different ~ the unique design on each tiny piece is revealed and we realise then that no group is faceless. I was swiftly reminded of how we can so easily put people and situations at a distance, claiming to 'know' them.

Once the pattern or order of anything is understood, the door is unlocked and a message is revealed. We need to slow down to see this message and encourage a perspective which rises above the duality of action and reaction, black and white, 'yes' or 'no'. Indeed, it was that wise Japanese philosopher, DT Suzuki, who, after becoming acquainted with Shakespeare's *Hamlet*, suggested the truth may be rather closer to, '...To be *and* not to be' rather than, '...To be *or* not to be.'

The best perspective we can aspire to is the Divine Perspective. The Divine is a Whole (Unity) embracing all things as 'wholes', whereas we tend to see things in 'part'. Hence, invariably we are limited by time, place and circumstance, unable to see the Divine Order which is transcendent and perfect. In truth, we can only see wholes when we too are whole.

Most of us know the 'Elephant story'... one person has the trunk and calls that the reality, whilst another person has the tail, and calls that reality, but it is *one* elephant! Problems arise when I insist that the elephant is the trunk and you insist that it is the tail! This is a major cause of all forms of fanaticism and intolerance. We need to unfold in consciousness in order to see things as wholes.

Prime ministers may change, nations may rise and fall, but let us not be deceived, Perfect Order is the timeless Order behind change. 'The Times They Are A-Changin'' sang Bob Dylan... in the realms of time this will always be the case, but let's ever be aware of the changeless nature of Eternity without which there could be no change.

Pause

Fall still. Come into your Centre and develop that inner vision which sees beyond the 'part' to the 'whole'.

Taking the Colours of the Day back into the White Light of Eternity

Amidst the apparent tumult of the world and, for many, the alarm, we know that it is more imperative than ever that we enter that Still Point within which gives us both our bearings and our perspective. Without anchoring ourselves in This, it is easy to become subject to the ravages of time and forget our timeless purpose as souls. 'Be still and Know that I am God' says Psalm 46:10. This text has cleverly been used as a chant to take us back to our essence in Being. I suggest that you try it for yourselves by chanting each line as follows:

Be still and Know that I am God
Be still and Know that I am
Be still and Know
Be still
BE

Grounded in the Light within, we become fixed in the Still Point which allows us to meet the ever-changing zeitgeist of the time and rejoice with it.

Throughout autumn and winter nature is disrobing and its stark reality is being revealed without frill or frippery. The beautiful attire of leaf, flower and fruit fall away and nothing can hide ~ all is laid bare. Gone is the daffodil trumpet of spring, gone is the perfume of summer roses in the breeze; gone is the mellow technicolour of autumn's rich raiment. Come are the cold winds, the short days, the long nights, the apparent barrenness of winter. All around there is a palpable stillness and silence.

Taking the Colours of the Day back into the White Light of Eternity

If you pass a beam of white light through a prism, the light splits into the colours of the rainbow. At the beginning of the year we start, as it were, with a blank white sheet. The events, the insights, the experiences of the year, are yet to come; each is like a colour, ready to spill out on to a pristine canvas. At the end of each year, invariably on New Year's Eve, we bring to mind the highlights of that year. But we don't have to wait for the end of the year; it is helpful to practise this at the end of each day, taking the 'colours' of each twenty-four hours back into the timeless calm of the White Light. The precise detail of our daily experience is not important. Rather, it is our capacity to meditate on the *essence* of those experiences that increases the wisdom within us ~ wisdom we can share.

Entering into the winter of ourselves where the soft light nurtures us and we are left alone to digest all that happened this year, I cannot help but think of that stable into which the Christ Light was born. This too was devoid of all the trappings of the world; it was silent ~ lit only by stars ~ and symbolises for us, perhaps, a place of tremendous humility. The Light is only born into the humble heart ~ a heart free in the flow of unconditional love ~ and to the soul who has understood that one by one words are left behind so that *Be Still and Know that I am God* becomes, *Be still and Know that I am* and then, *Be Still and Know,* and then *Be.* Just like all nature, it is time for us to uncloak and to take the experiences of the year into the 'stable' with us. It is 'here' that the stillness will heal us and the naked Presence will remind us of who we are. From this unadorned interior, I extend a warm hand to greet you.

> *Pause*
>
> At the end of each day, take the 'colours' ~ your experiences ~ back into the stillness and calm of the white Light within.
>
>

The Power of Creative Thinking ~ Collaboration in the Aquarian Age

It is true to say that much of what we do is in some sense creative, but to be truly creative we must bring the light of conscious intention to bear. In doing this we imitate our Source, which creates out of the super-conscious Knowing of Itself. It was the scientist and inventor of the telephone, Alexander Graham Bell, who said, *Concentrate all your thoughts upon the work in hand. The sun's rays do not burn until brought to a focus.* In the same vein, Thomas Alva Edison, the inventor of the first successful electric light bulb said: *I have far more respect for the person with a single idea who gets there than for the person with a thousand ideas who does nothing...* and to succeed, he commends the quality of *stick-to-it-ness*.

Invariably we think of creativity in terms of the pragmatic and expressive arts, such as DIY, dancing, singing or making something, and of course this is true. But meditating on the nature of the Pure Ideas behind all creation is even more potent since it is man's distinctive prerogative to think creatively and so touch the invisible Ideas behind the physical planes. With *intention*, even simple acts like seeing and listening are creative because they reveal aspects of the world and nuances that are not picked up if we are seeing and hearing with the common eye and ear. It is true to say that we can bring loving awareness to everything we see and do. This heightened awareness will reveal worlds within worlds ~ aspects of creation that we have not seen before. The insights arising from such vision are life-giving and often very joyful ~ we want to share them! This is the way that all collaborative creative projects grow.

If our creations are founded on *real* Ideas (Ideas like Goodness, Truth and Beauty, that are changeless), they have a dynamic and timeless quality, inspiring each soul who touches them.

Invariably, a project is 'birthed' or brought into the world when a number of souls work together to manifest different aspects of the whole. This is very much the spirit of the Aquarian Age ~ co-creation. History too has proved that this is how progress is made. For instance, the first electric light was made in 1800 by an English scientist, Humphry Davy. In 1860 it was perfected further by the English physicist, Sir Joseph Wilson Swan, who in 1878, displayed his new electric lamps in Newcastle and, in 1877, Charles Francis Brush used his knowhow to light a public square in Ohio, USA. It was Edison who eventually produced a bulb that could glow for 1500 hours. Lewis Howard Latimer, Will R Whitney and William David Coolidge went on to refine the light bulb further, finally producing the incandescent bulb.

It is true to say, though, that souls do not always collaborate. Sometimes there is dispute and rivalry and yet when the idea is fully birthed, perhaps many years or even centuries later, a coherent picture emerges which shows that each individual was responsible for taking it to a certain point before it is picked up by the next person. But the spirit of collaboration is to be applauded because it is based upon the recognition that we *all* have a part to play. It seems to me that we must live with passion and be ready and willing to serve and to collaborate. It was Alexander Graham Bell who said: *Great discoveries invariably involve the co-operation of many minds. I may be given credit for having blazed the trail, but when I look at the subsequent developments I feel the credit is due to other rather than to myself.* And Thomas Alva Edison echoes this: *A good idea is never lost. Even though its originator or possessor may die without publicizing it, it will some day be reborn in the mind of another.* And again Edison highlights the importance of service and collaboration: *The dove is my emblem... I want to serve and advance human life, not destroy it. I never perfect an invention that I did not think about in terms of the service it might give to others. I find out what the world needs, then I proceed to invent... I readily absorb ideas from every source, frequently starting where the last person left off.*

It may also be true to say that creativity allows us to rest from the burden of ourselves! When we are taken up with manifesting a creative idea, we find that the ego loosens its grip and the creative heartbeat is able to move through us more freely. So often when the light comes on within ourselves, we see a creation in a state of completeness after which comes much effort and 'blood, sweat and tears' in the working out of it. I think this comes from the endeavour to manifest the ideal onto a denser more physical plane, which is never 100 percent possible, hence our dissatisfaction with our creations! But we must keep trying because by doing so our creations can reflect more and more of heaven. Good luck with yours!

Pause

Cherish an insight today and share it with a friend or colleague.

The Infallible Workings of Justice

Such is the glory and majesty of the Ideal of Justice that we tend to take a deep breath before uttering a single word about it. Like all Divine Ideals, our definition of it will be limited by our own ignorance, but as we grow in consciousness, it will be seen more clearly. It would be easier to run away from such an examination, but let us be brave, slay the ugly monster of inertia and survey the land.

Socrates once asked a man, 'What is Virtue?' In reply he was given a whole host of delightful examples, 'I don't want a swarm of bees', he said, 'but the *essence* ~ what is common to them all.' Most of us are the same, we can think of many examples of justice (and therefore injustice), but what of Justice itself?

It is true that by collecting examples we can gain valuable insights into the nature of Justice, but there are other approaches too. One way is by considering symbols. In the West one of the better known symbols is Lady Justice. In the UK, the bronze statue of her atop the Old Bailey is well known. In her left hand she holds a pair of scales, in her right, a sword. She is blindfolded.

The symbol is generally female denoting that Justice resides in the bosom of Life and as Providence caters for all our needs, providing what is due and lawful and what is best for us. Divine Justice reigns supreme with an All-Knowing Eye which transcends time, place and circumstance. It sees the Whole, whereas we see only the part. The mortal part of us does not understand the workings of Providence and from our limited viewpoint, its ministrations may appear suspect or even downright unjust!

The fact that Lady Justice is blindfolded represents the impartial nature of Justice. The mortal eye, whose assessments are generally drawn from externals, is cut off. This reminds us to rely not so much on our outer vision, but to cultivate that inner vision which goes beyond the five senses and remains undisturbed by externals. Ultimately, because Providence cannot be known by the *finite* mind, we must learn to trust, accept, and co-operate with its ministrations, even when we cannot understand it. In order to see clearly, we must go beyond the merely cerebral and unfold the higher Mind with its intuitive-spiritual aspect and its grasp of wholenesses. This is a lifetime's work.

The blindfold also symbolises the Absolute nature of Justice which is not dependent upon anything external. It rules for the good of the whole and therefore, necessarily, for the good of each part. It is not influenced by humankind. If it were, it would be less than Absolute and would imply that part of it was deficient and open to amendment.

Some may ask, If the Divine is unmoved by us, what is the point of intercessionary prayer? This is when we pray to the Divine for a certain person, or a certain situation, to be healed. Invariably we believe that if our prayers are fervent enough, our pleas will somehow 'move' the Divine into action. Moreover, we do not always offer our prayers unconditionally, but pray that a situation may be resolved in a certain way. Although often well meant, there is great arrogance in this. As if the Divine needs to be informed as to the needs of any soul and how those needs might be met! But this is not to deny the importance of intercessionary prayer, as when we pray we are effectively opening a channel to the Divine, receiving Its healing balm and communicating that to those we hold in mind. We are, of course, all inextricably linked and in prayer we minister to each other.

The sword held by the figure of Justice symbolises the decisive nature of Divine Justice. Being omniscient, the Divine does not have to 'weigh things in the balance' as we do. There is absolute equity. For us the scales represent that prudence which looks at a situation impartially 'in the round' and comes to a decision.

The outworking of Justice always goes hand in hand with that other Divine Ideal ~ Mercy ~ as the ministrations of Providence are always merciful and compassionate. How could it be otherwise as there is nothing about us that that Great One does not know.

Pause

Trust that Justice is at work for your good and for the good of all.

Nourishing Our Whole Being

Most of us cannot fail to notice that many magazines and advertisements about healthy living concentrate almost exclusively on physical health and wellbeing ~ diet, exercise and the right cleansing programme. Moreover, in recent years the desire to look a certain way has accelerated and the cosmetic plastic surgery industry is burgeoning. Treatments like Botox are offered to diminish wrinkles and give a healthy appearance to the skin. Teeth are professionally whitened, or at least toothpastes proliferate purporting to do the same thing. There is nothing new about this. Men and women have always sought the 'body beautiful'. Fortunately, though, there has been a corresponding growth in holistic therapies addressing the *whole* person ~ spirit, soul and body. Because we are spiritual-corporeal beings, both aspects need to be taken into account.

On the whole it is much easier and less hard work to consider only our physical diets, but as spiritual beings, it is vital that we consider the nourishment of our souls or what we might term our metaphysical diet. Just as for our physical diets we need certain foods and minerals to keep ourselves in balance, so in the metaphysical diet there are essentials which promote health and wellbeing. These may be described differently by various traditions, but essentially they are:

- Right Aspiration
- Right Effort
- Right Earnestness
- Right Aims
- Right Valuation

- Right Purpose
- Right Teaching
- Right Knowledge
- Right Practice

In any 24-hour period, we may adopt all, or some, of these essentials. The more we can adopt, the greater balance we achieve. It may be helpful to ponder each one and keep pondering as insight builds on insight. The relationship between them is also helpful to consider.

Of course we are not absolved of the responsibility to give careful consideration to the physical side of our lives. These essentials apply to all aspects of life, physical as well as metaphysical.

Invariably, we consider *what* we take into our body and over the last few years, thankfully, we are considering more and more *where* our food comes from and the *manner of its production*. In addition, we might also consider what *we* contribute in the exchange of goods and services. Do we walk to our shops or do we drive? Are our purchases ethical ones and from ethical suppliers? Knowledge can help us in our quest and books like *The Good Shopping Guide* and *Save Cash and Save the Planet* are helpful. A few years back an advertisement by the magazine *Ethical Consumer* caught my eye... They feature a supermarket till roll receipt, headed up, *Who cares Saverstores*. A short extract reads as follows:

'Your checkout operator today is: Bored'

Wash up liquid -	eco unfriendly	0.65
Doz eggs -	factory farmed	0.85
Sgr snap peas -	low wage labour	0.47
Lrg. shampoo -	Animal tested	1.64
Designer trainer -	Oppress Regime	9.00
TOTAL		MESS

Fortunately, we have marvellous organisations and shining stars like Sir David Attenborough, Tony Juniper, Satish Kumar, Vandana Shiva, Greta Thunberg and Sir James Lovelock (who celebrated his 100th birthday in 2019), who are leading us back to our real work as good stewards of the planet.

Pause

Today find ways to nourish the inner and outer you and know that they are not separate.

The Fountain of Life ~ Singing our Note

Renewal is the keynote of spring, but is cyclic and a constant theme in the life of the soul. The fountain, or spring, is a fitting symbol of renewal. Waters well up abundantly from a single underground source. Spiritually, we might think of them as cascading in endless supply from the Heart of the divine Mother, quenching the thirst of man, bird and beast.

As a symbol of abundant supply and eternal life, it is little wonder that foundations are so often featured in depictions of paradise and form part of the architecture of the world's cities and palaces. One has only to recall the ornate fountains found in palaces and gardens like the beautiful Generalife Gardens of the Alhambra in Granada; the Alcazar Palace in Seville and the stately fountains of Versailles in Paris (even though finding enough water for his fountains was a constant concern for Louis XIV).

We are told that Carl Jung devoted much of his time to the study of fountain symbolism. He believed that a fountain placed centrally in a garden was a symbol of individuality, and that the central area could be regarded as a *temenos*, or hallowed area. This makes sense, as when we enter into our own inner temple or hallowed area, we breathe our native air and are fully ourselves. Moreover, it is 'There', our common Home, where we meet all other souls.

Clearly, water cannot flow through congested vessels. On a prosaic level, just think about what happens when a shower becomes clogged with limescale ~ the water will not flow. The only way to ensure free flow is to remove the scale. In terms of the soul, what causes the blockages are inordinations like pride, vanity, acquisitiveness and so on. As these overlay our authentic nature, we become parched and unhappy; our creativity is staunched. The only way to cleanse ourselves is through the purgative or cathartic arts: spiritual reading, prayer, meditation, contemplation and ritual. Bathed in these ~ the *Fons juventutis* or waters of eternal life ~ we emerge like Aphrodite from the sea, cleansed, refreshed and brimming over with Life Force. It is helpful to remember that as we express that Life Force, we are actually imitating Providence ~ Whose nature is to give and govern wisely, always at the appropriate time. This celebration of Life is the singing out of our own distinctive 'note' ~ just as at the Dawn Chorus each bird contributes its own peculiar song. And *sing up* we must!

When the soul enters the eternal Life Stream, the laws of time and space, which make perfect sense on the mundane plane of time and space, are transcended. For contrary to physical laws, we are told (Isaiah 40:31) that *they who wait upon the Lord... shall renew their strength; they shall mount up with wings as eagles; they shall run, and shall not be weary, and they shall walk and not faint.*

Again, in the mundane world we are aware that we simply cannot be 'all things to all men' and yet in the eternal there is no limitation ~ just like the Buddha, we can grow another arm which will meet each new situation as it arises. Symbolically, the figure of the jester, or fool, serves to remind us that even the foolish can teach the wise.

Pause

Let's add to the Dawn Chorus by singing out, with confidence, our own golden note.

The Joy of Meditation

'Hope' is the thing with feathers
That perches in the soul,
And sings the tune without the words,
And never stops at all,

And sweetest in the gale is heard;
And sore must be the storm
That could abash the little bird
That kept so many warm.

I've heard it in the chilliest land,
And on the strangest sea;
Yet, never, in extremity,
It asked a crumb of me.
Emily Dickinson

If you have enjoyed this poem, the chances are, you have already started to meditate. Meditation isn't difficult, but the most natural thing in the world. Many of us do it all the time without realising it. But like any science-art (and it is both), it is based upon timeless principles. When we follow those, we find our meditations more illuminating and truly refreshing.

The 'mark' of a good meditation is that it is rejuvenating ~ it fills us with life ~ and yet it is deeply calming and centring. The practice of meditation brings about these qualities because through it we learn to con-centrate (the word means, 'draw to a centre') which causes all our scattered energies to become focussed and re-aligned. Sometimes we may feel 'nervy' as if various parts of ourselves have been thrown up into the air and will not settle. This feeling of fragmentation is invariably born of too much activity or too many experiences piled on top of one another. In short, the failure to properly digest experiences leads to indigestion. Meditation can be used as a way of processing our experiences ~ that doesn't mean becoming bogged down in the detail, but rather entering a state of being which allows us to distil the precious essence from the 'heart' of our experiences. As anyone will know who has tried it, this cannot be achieved without a great deal of discipline.

Meditation could be described as a 'calm and simple pondering' or reflection. Like the tides of the sea or the heartbeat, ideally it has a 'pulse' ~ a subjective in-drawing followed by an objective out-pouring. It allows us to value the things born in time by helping us to ascend to their life-giving, immutable Ideas in the Mind of the Creator.

It is important to prepare for meditation. If you were entering a beautiful temple, would you not first take off your shoes, wash your hands and perhaps offer up a prayer? Preparation is therefore both physical and superphysical. So we might employ water and incense as cleansing agents and inspirational reading, prayer, meditation, contemplation and ritual to lift us up. It is also worth remembering that inspiring conversation with a friend (or within a discussion group) can be a good means of preparation and indeed may even lead to mutual meditation, the fruits of which can be increased insight, energy and the undertaking of joint projects.

In reality, every meditation has abiding (static-being), proceeding (dynamic-life) and returning (ideal-health) aspects. We ponder an aspect of Nature and, like the hummingbird, sip the nectar of its being, life and intelligence. We reflect on an idea which, if it is real, will have a power and dynamism all of its own. This dynamic aspect means that it will be life-enhancing and will generate many other ideas. The 'returning' aspect of meditation means that we reach a point of synthesis, or new understanding, which leads us back to a thing's essence or being.

Just as there is preparation at the beginning of a meditation, so there should be thanksgiving at the end. This completes the cycle and without it we cannot fully receive what is given.

Although in the 21st century meditation is often undertaken in order to release stress and deal with anxiety (all to the good), that is not its highest purpose. The highest goal of meditation is to come into touch with our Divine Source. The 20th Century thinker, HT Hamblin, called it entering into the 'Repose of the Infinite'. He describes this as, 'the stillness of unimpeded activity'. He uses the symbol of a globe on which are painted uneven concentric circles. However, once it is spun at great speed, the more perfect the circles appear. Imperfection is swallowed up by the speed at which the globe moves. And so, as we meditate, we enter into that everlasting Peace in which all the incidentals of our lives cease to have the overriding significance which we often give to them. Instead, they are seen in the context of the real and therefore their true significance is revealed.

Pause

Know that when you meditate, the 'small stuff' falls into perspective and is accorded no more than it deserves!

Finding the Divine by Accepting Ariadne's Golden Thread

Going back into the mists of time alchemists have been in pursuit of what is called the *Philosopher's Stone*. This precious Stone could not only turn base metal into gold but could also cure disease and even prolong life. Sir Isaac Newton is perhaps the world's most famous alchemist and he wrote extensively on the subject. Whilst I am not ruling out that it may be literally possible to transform base metal into gold (on the basis that as artist-souls at work in the cosmos, we possess those same elements and can work with them in a creative process), alchemy as a spiritual metaphor is more interesting. On this inner level the base metals represent our earthy natures which when transformed by the 'gold' within us ~ the spirit ~ are uplifted and work as true servants, co-operating with spirit, and being led by it.

When, by the perfecting action of Divine Grace, in conjunction with our own efforts, the gold within us is revealed, what follows is really what Jesus called the 'second birth'. He said (John 3:3), *I say unto thee, except a man be born again, he cannot see the Kingdom of God.* To all intents and purposes, this is really when we become truly human, having formerly survived on a purely instinctual level. Indeed, it is possible to pass a whole lifetime operating on an instinctual level. There is no judgement in this, but it is state of profound sleep.

It is only possible to unite with something when we become like it. The mysterious process of Alchemy sees the soul as a crucible in which all our elements receive the touchpaper of the Divine Fire. As they burn, there is a purification and eventually what is left is seen to be only the real ~ pure gold. By realising consciously that the essence of our nature is divine, we can become what the sages have called 'Friends of God'. The implications of this are momentous, as it points to a relationship with the Divine which is as 'Friend to friend' rather than superior to inferior. Then it becomes possible to rise above the purely natural level of human experience and join hands, as it were, with the celestials, which are God in his manifestation. This idea is encapsulated in Psalm 8:5 where it says that the Son of Man is 'but little lower than the Elohim.' The word 'Elohim' is somewhat ambiguous but could be translated as 'the gods' (Aspects of God). The implications are profound: once we have 'put on' the Christ nature, our union with the Divine will transform us to such a degree as to make us co-creators with It.

Alchemy can operate at all levels of our being. By meditating on absolute Ideals (like Unity, Goodness, Beauty and Truth) and walking their truth, our lives gradually blossom and unfurl, like the petals of a lotus blossom. In Alchemy, our ideas, some of which we may have held for decades, undergo a refining process in the fires of meditation and lived experience. As mental alchemists, we look within and behind the seen to the unseen; we go from the apparent and seeming to the truly knowable and certain. It is as if we put on glasses that enable us to have X-ray vision, seeing through to the true nature of things and situations. In this sense we gradually become masters of the art of symbolism, honouring the physical nature of things but knowing that their visible semblance ~ colour, shape, taste, fragrance, texture ~ is but a diluted reflection of their divine inner essence. In meditation, we can touch that essence and because it is divine, we are lifted up into pure Beauty. Having touched it, we become artist-souls wishing to imitate it and create our own beautiful things! These beautiful children inspire other souls to create and so more beautiful children are raised in the world and the reign of Beauty continues.

As aspiring souls, many of us thirst for that beauty we once knew so intimately when we were free of the earthly vestment. But now, in incarnation, it is for us as artist-souls to bring heaven to earth and earth to heaven.

The English poet, Francis Thompson, describes this challenge well in his poem, 'The Kingdom of God':

O world invisible, we view thee,
O world intangible, we touch thee,
O world unknowable, we know thee,
Inapprehensible, we clutch thee!

Spiritual literature, including prose, parable, fable, myth and poetry ~ all employ simile and metaphor to describe the Path and the challenges we meet on the way. This corpus of wisdom cannot be over estimated. We can learn much from reading these works, as within them our own dilemmas and challenges are 'writ large'. In truth, they provide the Golden Threads which lead us safely out of our labyrinths.

> *Pause*
>
> *The importance of spiritual literature cannot be over estimated since it teaches us about our own challenges and dilemmas.*
>
> *Ariadne gives Theseus a Golden Thread so that he can find his way out of the labyrinth.*
>
>

A Rainbow of Abundance

Every season is clothed with abundance in different, special, ways, but at no time is this more evident than in the spring when the multiplicity of green shoots makes such a strong contrast to the apparent barrenness of winter. Peaking through comes the fragile Galanthus, or snowdrop, adorning gardens and woodland with seventy-five different species of its pretty milky white flowers. The primrose, that 'firstling of the infant year', manifests its abundance in more than five hundred species. The daffodil, clothed with the sun, is a familiar 'trumpet' of spring. There are at least twenty-five species of these yellow glories and over thirteen thousand hybrid varieties. But the picture would be incomplete without the human soul who witnesses all this. She finds meaning in Nature because of the Ideas woven through it which she also shares. For instance, at a simple level, all of Nature has a self-preserving aspect (if there is danger, it withdraws), a self-assertive aspect (it works to hold its space and power) and a communicative aspect (it reveals itself through colour, fragrance, texture, taste and sound). We, too, possess these together with other faculties, like Reason and Intuition, which make us truly human.

As artist-souls at work in the world of the four elements, we are not only able to offer wise stewardship of our home, but make music by drawing together these elements and creating an extra, quintessentially human, dimension. This is through the application of various works of art, be they pragmatic and expressive, like DIY or dance, or ordinative, theoretic or mystical ~ like medicine, philosophy and prayer.

In raising natural beauty to a super-natural level, we are very much like the god Hermes (or Mercury), the conductors or mediums for this to take place.

Consciously, or unconsciously, we are all engaged in this work. Although we are influenced by the same forms in Nature, we create in a beautiful rainbow of different ways. So again, there is an abundance of creations ~ single ideas and ideals being celebrated in countless ways. This is clearly reflected in our own bodies (and in the bodies of Nature). Although we all share the same basic components, there is infinite variety in the way those components are put together.

Imitating Nature we give unconditionally as well as abundantly ~ without expectation of reward. To imitate Nature we must touch her invisible soul. Dr Stephan Harding, Coordinator of the MSc in Holistic Science at Schumacher College, and author of *Animate Earth: Science, Intuition and Gaia*, talks about encountering Nature in a way which goes beyond intellectual process. He says, *...Its conceptual structure vanishes and you actually meet each being as coming forth from itself as itself, revealing itself to you in a way which is beyond your intellect ~ much more deeply*. It is an intuitive encounter which can perhaps best be framed through poetry. Stephan has had much experience of this type of encounter through his work with Muntjac deer, which he studied for his Doctorate.

As we give, we become open to the abundance all around us and contribute to it. It is said that the only external act of God is to give, so in giving we not only imitate Nature but we also emulate our Source.
'Give and it shall be given unto you; good measure, pressed down, and shaken together, and running over, shall men give into your bosom.' (Luke 6:38). All the world's great teachings agree on this ~ the more we give, the more we become able to receive. Perhaps because in giving there is a self-emptying that makes it possible to truly receive.

Pause

Encountering the abundance of Nature, we can go beyond our own conceptual framework and meet the essence of each being. It is a soul encounter.

Let's Say 'Yes' to Life

It is said that overcoming fear is an important initiation and a great achievement. Most of us would readily assent to this statement, but very few of us will have attained it. Underlying anxiety and niggling worries can so easily undermine our lives, affecting every area. Hence the rise in Mindfulness and other techniques which help us to deal with this.

Undoubtedly, some of the anxiety is not generated by us but by the collective, from the mass of radio, television, newspaper and internet reporting which not only exacerbates our fears but also lives by feeding off our own negative energy. This is precisely what happens when we pass on a news story in a negative way, perhaps embellishing sad facts in order to heighten their impact. It might be better if we could find a seed of the positive in it and pass that on.

Fear feeds on fear, so it seems important to rise above it to where love resides and meet the fear with that. Fear contracts and we go into a shell which prevents us getting out and others getting in. The antidote is pure love, which melts away the shell and lets us out. In the face of its power and warmth, the cold night of fear dissipates, unable to live in its presence.

Prayer can be seen as an expression of love. When we hear about catastrophes in the world and experience difficulty in own lives and watch others facing challenges, we can best meet them not by turning away, but through prayer. We can pray that we might be given the strength to cope with whatever arises. When you think about your troubles or witness those in the lives of others, just stop whatever you are doing for a moment and offer up a prayer.

Again, if there is a challenge on the horizon or we need help dealing with a particular situation, let's offer up a prayer.

It seems important to hold constantly before us the Socratic injunction, 'Man, Know Thy Self'. In reality, this is our only salvation. Ultimately, everyone must take up this injunction and, by doing so, break through all ignorance and darkness.

Fears are generated by unhealthy thinking. They have no substance but are merely phantasms ~ shadowy apparitions ~ projected onto the view-finder of the mind. It is we that breathe life into them and then believe them. Invariably, these ghosts are born from a negative sequence of 'what ifs'... *What if I take that job but I'm not up to it? What if I move house but find it doesn't suit me? What if I become ill and unable to cope?* Lack of faith, both in ourselves and in others, seems to stop us in our tracks ~ we desperately need it if we are to move forward. Prudence too is essential, as it helps us to know where best to direct our energies and wisely take stock. But most of all, we need the wisdom and guidance of our Guardian Angel. It important to ask for help. So settle down into the Silence of your inner Self and ask. The answer may not come in your time, but it will come. Again, it may not come in the way you envisage, but it will come. Try to find time to withdraw every day and listen for that inner prompting which is invariably the answer to a prayer.

Fear can mar, and indeed, abort, any creative enterprise. In mythology this is graphically symbolised by the god Saturn swallowing his children. It is the equivalent of floating a positive idea ~ *what if I ran in that race?* Or, *what if I wrote that book?* ~ and then extinguishing it through fearful thoughts of not being strong enough or clever enough. Such is the insidious power of negative thinking ~ it can take away our zest for life and edge us into smaller and smaller spaces. It is true that we may not succeed in worldly terms, but we must try to dwell on only the positive, knowing that nothing is wasted and that what we learn from our so-called failures may greatly outweigh what we learn from our successes!

Pause

Today face the fear and go forward knowing that you are forever loved.

Flexibility

On warm, sunny days I like to watch the Silver Birch in my garden dance in the breeze. This puts me in mind of the words of Jesus, as recorded by St John: *The wind bloweth where it listeth, and thou hearest the sound thereof, but canst not tell whence it cometh and whither it goeth: so is everyone that is born of the Spirit.* No one has ever seen the wind, but it is nonetheless always with us. As Jesus says, we cannot tell where it comes from and where it goes. And so, everyone born again of the Spirit is mysteriously present when circumstances demand it, but able to move on freely when obligations are fulfilled. In this way there is no attachment ~ only the concern that we fulfil our purpose in any given situation.

The soul that is able to move 'as the wind listeth' is, in reality, a master of all space and time, able to stand atop the mountain, witness the signs of the times and judge precisely what is needed and when.

The movement of the wind can range all the way through from a cooling, gentle breeze to a life-threatening hurricane or tornado. But, whatever it brings, we must be prepared to meet and welcome it. Poetically we talk about the winds of change blowing through our lives. Invariably it is these which move us closer to the Infinite when our lives become stuck or stale. Sometimes this is because we have become overly attached to the letter or form of our lives at the expense of the living spirit coursing through it. It is rather like a river becoming dammed up by old branches and debris ~ the flow of the water is hindered. Such is the power and adaptability of water, invariably it finds a way through, but it is not the most direct route. One could say that obstructions make us stronger and this is often true, but at the same time, the life within us needs to be directed and to flow freely so we can accomplish our purposes effectively. This is not to say that there will not be external challenges, but rather that we have the power and life flowing through us to meet them. The answer is always to 'plug in' back to our Source, for It is Life and Power. A crude and somewhat limited example of this is battery power ~ when we fail to plug our home appliances and laptops into the mains, energy begins to diminish, runs low and finally the equipment will not work any more.

Wind, as well as water, has cleansing properties. Strong winds can remove obstacles. We can choose to resist the wind, firmly buttoning our coats, putting our hands in our pockets and stoically putting our heads down to avoid it. On the other hand, we can allow a bracing wind to lift us and blow all the cobwebs away.

Just as the wind changes direction, so do the choices and challenges that present themselves to us. One minute we are heading east when suddenly, without warning, a situation blows in from the west and we must change direction to meet it. It is important that we are ready to act sensitively to meet each situation as it unfolds, but this is only possible when we are centred in our Source which is the 'Still Point' above and beyond all space and time. By coming close to our Source we can be sure that no matter the direction of the wind, we shall not be knocked off balance. Moreover, operating from our centre, our actions will be more enlightened and free of self.

The wind may also blow away aspects of our lives which are no longer serving us. This implies a trust in the capacity of the wind to carry us and to make way for the new. If not, we tend to struggle and suffer. Yes, we have to work to re-align ourselves, but we also have to trust. Look at the glider in the sky, not reliant on an engine, but on thermals of air which give lift and allow it to spiral upward.

Birds do not rely solely on flapping their wings to migrate; they would become exhausted and surely perish. Instead they glide on the wind, and are thus able to travel vast distances in search of warmer climates. Relying on the Divine at all times lifts us out of exhaustion and into the warm thermals and the blue sky where we can see more clearly.

Flexibility

Pause

Know that the Divine is the Power House of Strength and Wisdom to which you can turn whenever you like.